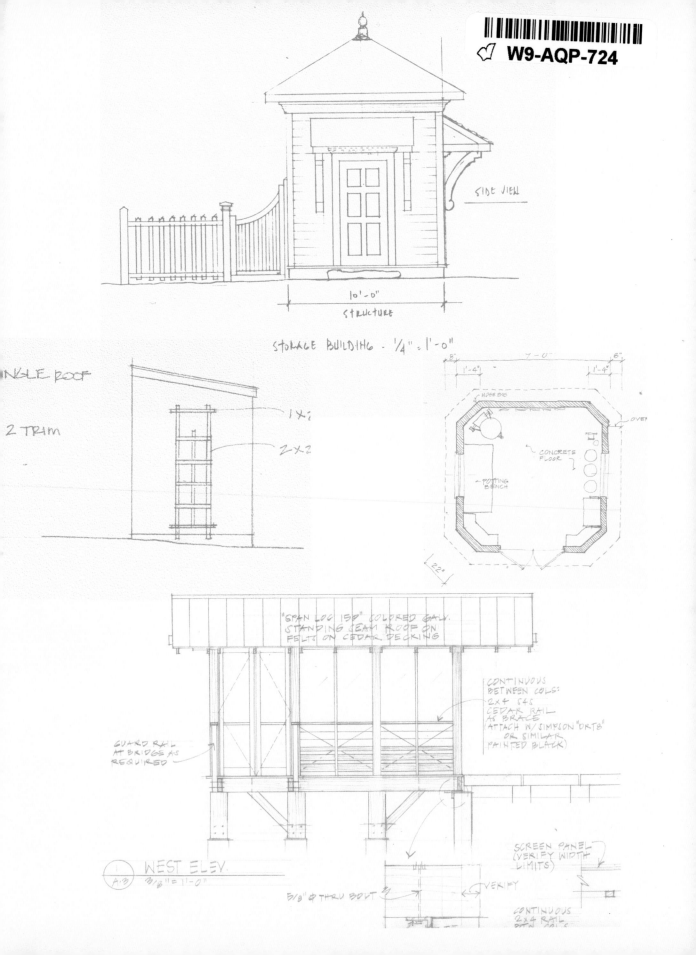

SIDE VIEW

10'-0"
STRUCTURE

STORAGE BUILDING - ¼" = 1'-0"

SHINGLE ROOF

2 TRIM

1x?
2x2

HOSE BIB

CONCRETE FLOOR

POTTING BENCH

OVER

22"

8"   7'-0"   8"
1'-4"   1'-4"

"SPAN LOC 150" COLORED GALV.
STANDING SEAM ROOF ON
FELT; ON CEDAR DECKING

CONTINUOUS
BETWEEN COLS:
2x4 S4S
CEDAR RAIL
AS BRACE
(ATTACH W/ SIMPSON "DRT8"
OR SIMILAR
PAINTED BLACK)

GUARD RAIL
AT BRIDGE AS
REQUIRED

SCREEN PANEL
(VERIFY WIDTH
LIMITS)

WEST ELEV.
3/16" = 1'-0"
A·3

5/8" Ø THRU BOLT

VERIFY

CONTINUOUS
2x4 RAIL

STYLISH SHEDS AND ELEGANT HIDEAWAYS

STYLISH SHEDS AND ELEGANT HIDEAWAYS

Debra Prinzing

PHOTOGRAPHS BY WILLIAM WRIGHT

Clarkson Potter/Publishers

New York

With love and gratitude to my incredibly supportive husband, Bruce Brooks, and our sons, Benjamin Michael Brooks and Alexander Morgan Brooks. "It" happened! And to Bill Wright, the best and most talented collaborator a writer could ever hope to have.

—DP

With love and thanks to my wife, Pauline, and our daughter, Ella, for their love, encouragement, and patience throughout this project. And to my parents, Will and Nancy, who have been supportive since the very beginning, and Debra Prinzing, who has been a great producer, stylist, fellow traveler, and friend.

—WW

PAGE 1: A basket filled with lavender and golden tickseed (*Coreopsis* sp.) greets visitors to Lani Freymiller's cottage courtyard. PAGE 2: A vintage window suspended from an arbor in Sylvia and Steven Williams's Texas garden creates an inviting outdoor room. PAGE 3: One of two dragonfly brackets on the front of the children's playhouse in Kathy and Ed Fries's garden holds a container planted with raspberry-colored twinspur (*Disacia* sp.) and black mondo grasses. OPPOSITE: Interior designer Betty Wasserman displays an untitled series by photographer Lisa Ross across a ledge inside her garage-turned-guest-cottage in Southampton, New York.

Clarkson N. Potter is a trademark and Potter and colophon are registered trademarks of Random House, Inc.

Library of Congress Cataloging-in-Publication Data has been applied for.

ISBN 978-0-307-35291-0

Printed in Singapore

Design by Marysarah Quinn

10 9 8 7 6 5 4 3 2 1
FIRST EDITION

ENDPAPER ARCHITECTURAL DRAWINGS: Top row, from left: copyright © Gregory Thomas (tea house); copyright © Brad McGill, Ellis Landesign (storage building). Middle row, from left: copyright © Jean Zaputil, Jean Zaputil Garden Design (garden plan and potting shed); copyright © Gregory Bader, Bader Architecture (garden shed floor plan). Bottom row, from left: copyright © Gregory Bader, Bader Architecture (garden shed); copyright © Gregory Thomas (tea house).

CONTENTS

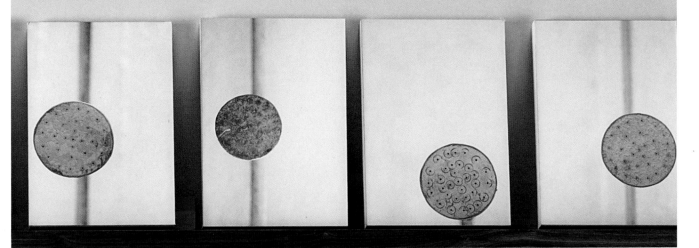

ESCAPE
TO YOUR
OWN
BACKYARD

FOWLER
CREEK
HOLLOW

Virginia Woolf had it right. Women (and men, it turns out) yearn for a room of their own. But instead of a little nook beneath the eaves, that room is now a shed. And it is located outdoors, in the backyard, where it serves as an alluring destination for endeavors both practical and passionate.

What then is a shed exactly? Traditionally defined, the shed is considered a small structure, either freestanding or attached to a larger building, open-sided or with a door. For centuries, it has served a purpose for storage or temporary shelter.

After visiting more than one hundred sheds around the country and meeting their owners and creators, I crafted a contemporary definition that suits this term. *Today's shed is a small structure designed and built for one's personal enjoyment.*

Sublime and seductive, the shed has moved far beyond its quaint, utilitarian origins on the farm. Elevated to a new role that responds to and reflects the way we live, it is no longer an ugly duckling hidden away in a corner of the yard next to the compost bin. A colorful crop of sheds populates suburban gardens, urban backyards, and country villages. These smart structures and artful havens evoke the lifestyles of their owners, fulfilling many roles beyond

tending to tomato starts and basil seedlings or hanging the rake and spade.

This new generation of small-scale, usually freestanding buildings represents something more dynamic in the twenty-first-century landscape. Called by many names—garden house, architectural folly, urban hut, modern hideaway—it can be an escape, a retreat, a sanctuary, an art studio, a dining room, or even a whimsical playhouse for all ages. It's where we showcase our personalities and preferences. Its modest size belies the abundant joy its occupants feel when they enter to sip tea, enjoy a glass of wine, admire the garden view, draw, paint, write poetry, daydream, nap, share secrets, or laugh with friends.

Dusted off and spruced up, the once-humble building displays architectural charm. Imagine the most appealing environment to suit your needs: begin with four walls, a roof, a door, a window or two. Inside, you can outfit a few hundred

OPPOSITE: Janie and Billy Fowler re-created a vintage waterwheel house, complete with shake siding, cobblestone edging, and a tin roof. Adorned with a yellow climbing rose that echoes the landscape's golden and orange flowering palette, the 8-by-8-foot structure gives their entry garden a point of view.

square feet of space with comfortable seating or a place to recline, ample lighting, and shelves or counters for displaying treasures, as well as hang artwork on the walls and play music to personalize your space.

Maybe your shed has its own front porch or a sleeping loft, or it's on stilts above a knot garden. Perhaps its furnishings reflect the style and palette of your home's interiors, or it holds cherished hand-me-downs and antiques. Its environment may be minimalist, where prayer, meditation, or daydreaming is nurtured. Highly personal, the modern shed is a selfish indulgence meant to be enjoyed.

The human need for a separate place appears in literature, speaking to the ideal of "sanctuary" in our personal lives. In his book *The Poetics of Space*, the French philosopher Gaston Bachelard wrote, "The recollection of moments of confined, simple, shut-in space are experiences of heartwarming space, of a space that does not seek to become extended, but would like above all still to be possessed . . . [it] is at once small and large, warm and cool, always comforting."

Bachelard's thoughts on shelter resonate with me, as do the words of architect Ann Cline, who calls her backyard shed a "hut." In her book of essays, *A Hut of One's Own*, Cline describes a journey taken by many of us (if only in our dreams): "Nowadays, the woman—or man—who wishes to experience the poetry of life . . . might be similarly advised to have a hut of her—or his—own. Here, isolated from the wasteland and its new world saviors, a person might gain perspective on life and the forces that threaten to smother it. Only

BELOW: Built from salvaged shingles and boards to suggest a turn-of-the-twentieth-century outbuilding, Janie and Billy Fowler's 8-by-8-foot potting shed is nearly obscured by vigorously growing akebia and clematis vines at the height of summer. Nestled in the far corner of their property, the miniature barn reflects their passion for raising ornamental and edible plants, collecting antiques, and displaying primitive agricultural implements.

in a hut of one's own can a person follow his or her own desires—a rigorous discipline. . . . Here, a person may find one's very own self, the source of humanity's song."

While poetically appealing, a shed or separate structure is also highly practical. We erect and decorate these small-scale buildings as an extension of our principal living areas. The designs incorporate diverse architectural finishes and iconic elements. Unique regional styles and innovative, often eclectic, uses of building materials and construction methods are employed. In the hands of artists, carpenters, and designers, the little backyard shed is a highly personal means of expression, one that reveals our yearning for escape and sanctuary.

To my friend John Akers, a Seattle carpenter and self-described "glorified recycler" who has designed and custom-built dozens of backyard sheds in the past decade (including sheds featured in "Island Idyll" and "Suburban Follies"), these *reimagined* shacks have attained a higher purpose. "I've seen so many situations where people have slowed down because of adding a shed to their property," John observes. "They experience something intangible when entering their sheds. Maybe it transports them to a simpler time."

What this carpenter-philosopher has to say makes a lot of sense. The modern shed may be a purely practical solution that expands the square footage of one's living space, or it may be a simple sanctuary in the garden. But either way, it is a gift. John sums up his observations with a laugh: "I guess you could say my motto is 'build a shed and change your life.'"

Inspired by the creators

BELOW: Designer Harrison Bates used ordinary greenhouse material such as steel studs and polycarbonate siding to create an extraordinary garden structure for his sister Loretta Fischer. The 430-square-foot shed is a winter greenhouse for potted tropical plants. Come summer, Loretta and her husband, Terrill, transform their "mod pod" for backyard entertaining, inviting friends for libations, and to dangle their toes in the refreshing moatlike pool.

and owners of thirty incredible spaces, *Stylish Sheds and Elegant Hideaways* explores the contemporary role of this once-humble structure. It offers inspiration and encourages imagination. William Wright's breathtaking and intimate photography captures the private spaces of people whose most gratifying hours are spent just steps away from the back door—whether they are pursuing horticulture, art, meditation, play, or entertainment.

My interviews with shed owners offer a snapshot of their lives—and reveal the individual pursuits, passions, and purposes that inspired their sheds. Architects, interior designers, landscape designers, and builders explain the decisions and choices they made during the design process. The narrative offers practical tips for selecting architectural details, choosing an exterior palette to complement the garden, or furnishing the interiors.

As you read about the nostalgic notions, vacation memories, and literary passages that inspired the featured shed designs, I encourage you to begin envisioning your own "perfect" shed setting. It's a completely self-indulgent exercise that requires you to imagine why, how, and where you can establish a private getaway to satisfy your desires.

Last spring I posed the question: "What's your dream shed and how will you use it?" to my audience at the San Francisco Flower and Garden Show, and I passed out index cards inviting people to jot ideas and make sketches. I was thrilled with the clever, innovative, and heartfelt suggestions offered that day. Many addressed

sensible or even frivolous space solutions, and all evoked a personal wish for individual expression. Here are some of my favorite ideas: a quilter's haven, a garden reading room, a yoga retreat, an entertainment hub, and a gallery for displaying thirty birdhouses.

As you dream about a shed of your own, take note of the practical and workable ideas featured in each chapter. In revealing their mission and must-have requirements for a backyard structure, each owner addresses the essential steps—from brainstorming and designing to constructing and decorating—to create an unforgettable private destination. Each chapter addresses practicalities such as site challenges and clever solutions, and provides a list of building materials. Armed with these resources and seduced by the photography of architecture, interior design, and finishing details, you may realize just how possible it is to make your vision a reality.

At the end of the book, I've listed resources for building materials, furnishings, accessories and art, blueprints, and finishing details. My goal was for each chapter to bring you closer to creating and enjoying a stylish shed of your own.

Stylish Sheds and Elegant Hideaways invites discovery and experimentation as gardeners, artists, designers, and individuals share how they have fashioned backyard destinations where sacred and inspirational moments are celebrated in everyday life. Enjoy the journey as you escape to your own outdoors.

OPPOSITE: The orange-streaked feather of a resident flicker is tucked between the wall studs in Terry and Dave Maczuga's "creek house."
FOLLOWING PAGES: Mary Martin keeps on her desk a framed photograph of the pink playhouse of her childhood. Positive memories of the small structure inspired her to renovate a backyard shed for her studio.

STYLISH SHEDS AND ELEGANT HIDEAWAYS

AN ARTISTIC DESTINATION

"The real reason my shed exists is so that I can work uninterrupted. There is no phone, no Internet in here."

—AMY BLOOM

When the diffused morning sun streams through a window, washing the canvas with its soft glow, or when the only sounds are the tap of fingers on a keyboard or the swish of a pencil being pulled across the drafting board, the artist is lost in the moment. The setting may be quiet, or there may be music playing, but the atmosphere is filled with intense concentration.

Regardless of their craft, poets, painters, designers, printmakers, writers, and composers require a place that's separate from the routine demands of everyday life.

What are the essentials? The occupant merely requires a door to close, windows to illuminate, a comfortable chair, and an easel or a desk.

The "shed" is an ideal outlet for the work of an artist. A studio, an office, an atelier, or a workshop—either placed in the heart of the garden or perhaps hidden far away from the main living quarters—is the incubator for creation. When an artist is uninterrupted and able to focus wholly on his or her technique, the muse is at work; inspiration flows freely. The artist's private space nurtures and sustains a life of creative expression.

STUCCO
STUDIO

A NEGLECTED GARAGE GETS A FACE-LIFT AS A USEFUL OFFICE, TURNING A DARK CORNER OF A SANTA MONICA GARDEN INTO A DAZZLING FOCAL POINT FOR PEOPLE AND PLANTS

Tired of crowding his landscape architecture practice into a tiny spare bedroom of his bungalow, Joseph Marek renovated a 400-square-foot garage. He's quadrupled his work space and created an attractive destination in the garden.

OPPOSITE: Joseph Marek and John Bernatz's paprika-colored studio is cooled by a crisp white trim on cottage-style windows and doors. Where the original asphalt driveway once stood is a gravel "carpet," edged in black pebbles. Retro seating upholstered in lime and orange outdoor fabric echoes the citrus palette inside. ABOVE: The men found the exotic-looking tribal head at a local flea market. PAGE 17: Joseph designed the chartreuse bookcases to form the perimeter of two work stations and accommodate drafting and computer activities. Melon- and apricot-colored walls infuse the room with energy.

During a garden tour featuring Joseph Marek and John Bernatz's lush Santa Monica landscape, a visitor was overheard gushing: "It's like stepping into heaven."

That sentiment puts a smile on the men's faces, giving them the satisfaction of knowing that their digging, planting, pruning, and design efforts have not gone unnoticed. "It's always fun to see how people react when they walk into our garden," says John, the household's self-described chief of maintenance.

The frequently toured garden is a labor of love for John and his partner, Joseph, the principal of Joseph Marek Landscape Architecture. Every square inch of this 50-by-150-foot city lot has been thoughtfully landscaped and decorated with fountains, sculpture, furniture, and, of course, plants.

MISSION
To convert an unused stucco garage from the 1930s into a light-filled backyard office

MUST-HAVES
French doors, windows, skylights, built-in desks, drafting tables, storage and bookcases, a seating area, and interesting lighting

INSPIRATION
To get just the right color of paint, Joseph had the hardware store match a jar of paprika from his spice cabinet.

DESIGN CHALLENGES
The bare garage lacked insulation and had an old concrete floor as well as a ceiling covered in layers of grime. Its only light source was from the doorway.

CREATIVE SOLUTIONS
A skylight in the darkest corner of the garage, two sets of French doors, and twin 36-by-60-inch cottage-style windows flood the interior with light from multiple sources. Original ceiling beams, now stripped and left natural, are warm and attractive. Power-washed and dressed with throw rugs, the concrete floor also remains.

ABOVE LEFT: Joseph uses the studio's exterior walls as a vertical gallery to showcase favorite plants, including these regal staghorn ferns. RIGHT: When John collects, he prefers mid-century artwork and objects, such as the 1960s-era Jeré sculpture of dozens of shiny metal discs. The quirky "pearl" lamp was a vintage shop find.

OPPOSITE, LEFT: Horticultural publications and nursery catalogs share the counter with a collection of vintage spray nozzles. Joseph fashioned the red "twig" pyramid as a scale model for a set of larger twig plant supports—also painted glossy red—for a client's vegetable garden. RIGHT: Orange accents appear throughout the office, both in a file box and a bird of paradise floral arrangement.

Since purchasing the restored 1938 stucco house, a classic three-bedroom bungalow that Santa Monica is known for, Joseph and John have not needed to do much more than paint its exterior walls butterscotch yellow and blood orange and decorate its interiors with their modern furnishings and art. Like most Californians, they filled the garage with boxes and "old, unloved, unused stuff," says John, who owns a travel agency. Joseph, who studied architecture as a Yale undergraduate and earned a master's in landscape architecture from the University of Virginia, divided the yard into a garden of distinct spaces, including intimate gravel courtyards, a sunny tropical garden, and a sunken outdoor "living room" situated beneath the leafy canopy of a stately Chinese elm. As embellishments, he and John have designed bubbling fountains, arranged sculpture and found objects, and displayed extensive plant collections (among their favorites: a rose cutting garden representing the full spectrum of the rainbow, silvery blue and gray tillandsias, heat-loving cacti and succulents, orchids, and staghorn ferns).

This garden plays a large role in Joseph and John's lives, so it is ironic that few of the rooms of their house overlook it. Yes, they can peek through a tiny window in the powder room or two small windows in the den, but in order to really enjoy the view, they have to walk outdoors.

In one corner of the garden stood the 400-square-foot garage, an underused structure with a slightly pitched roof and a pull-up door. The driveway had long since been appropriated for garden space and an outdoor dining area, so you couldn't park a car there even if you wanted to, Joseph points out.

In 2001, when he left a prominent landscape design firm to start his solo practice, Joseph actually tried working in the garage. But he was miserable inside the dark, cold structure. "So I decided to work in the small spare bedroom and was forced to use the bed as my drafting and layout table," he admits. "That lasted a year, but I knew I wasn't going to be able to do it much longer."

> "When I'm standing at the drafting table drawing, I think how nice it is that I get to see my garden while I'm working, rather than being in an office cubicle or a building with fluorescent lights."
>
> —JOSEPH MAREK

OWNERS
Joseph Marek and John Bernatz

DESIGN

ARCHITECTURE: Joseph Marek

LANDSCAPE: Joseph Marek

INTERIOR: Joseph Marek and John Bernatz

He returned to the garage, but this time with plans to transform it into an inspiring place where his design concepts would flourish. Joseph saw its potential for a light-filled studio overlooking the garden. "I knew what I wanted to fit in here. I needed at least two large desks—one for me and a future assistant, flat files for storing drawings, and space for books," he explains.

The original garage door was removed to make way for tandem 6-foot, 8-inch doors and a cottage-style window trimmed in white. This pairing continued on the garage's south wall, which overlooks the sunken garden at the back of the lot. "We used long, horizontal mullions on the doors and windows to match the windows on our house," Joseph says. He and John considered replacing or covering the garage's concrete floor and open-beam ceiling, but both elements required little more than refinishing. Cleaned and sealed, and covered with throw rugs, the floor's earthy patina is attractive. The overhead beams, stripped and left unfinished, add character to the ceiling.

Joseph selected apricot for the new interior walls and finished an accent wall in a slightly darker mango shade. He continued the citrus palette, painting the two U-shaped desks chartreuse; the inside sections of the built-in bookcases are tinged lavender.

Joseph and John wanted an earthy color for the office exterior. "I literally went into the kitchen spice cabinet and pulled

TOP: Joseph moved his landscape architecture practice from a spare bedroom to his converted garage, where he is surrounded by joy-inducing color, beloved plants, and his canine companions, including Pablo. ABOVE: One of a collection of one hundred silvery blue and gray tillandsias, also known as air plants, is displayed in perfect contrast to the vibrant stucco exterior.

a canister of paprika off the shelf. Then we matched it to paint chips to get the color right," Joseph says. The successful choice coordinates nicely with the original red terra-cotta roof tiles.

On any given day, Joseph leaves for work, which is just a few steps from his back door. Unless he is distracted by an interesting bloom or surprised by a hummingbird as it zings through the garden in search of nectar, he arrives at the studio within seconds. He's usually shadowed by canine companions Cooper and Pablo, who fill their days alternately taking a circuit around the garden's perimeter or napping on a cushion beneath Joseph's desk.

If friends or clients arrive, Joseph greets them in the studio "foyer," an outdoor seating area created when the driveway was leveled and terraced. The refreshing space is furnished with retro seating, upholstered in lime green outdoor fabric, a small ottoman that doubles as a cocktail table, and a lush backdrop of plants. The floor has a pebble carpet, a rectangle of green-hued gravel edged with a band of smooth black Mexican river rocks. "It's my reception area," Joseph points out. "I see people come through the gate and meet them here."

The studio does double duty as a place to entertain. A small built-in refrigerator provides refreshments; the men's kitchen is nearby, should a gathering increase in size. They appreciate the irony that this ex-garage is larger than any room in the house. "We hang out in here a lot," John says. "It has seating for everyone." Work space by day, party space by night, the studio is also an important garden element, Joseph adds. "It serves a good purpose. When I'm standing at the drafting table drawing, I think how nice it is that I get to see my garden while I'm working, rather than being in an office cubicle or a building with fluorescent lights."

MATERIALS

ROOF: Spanish-style red terra-cotta tile (original)

EXTERIOR: stucco (custom paprika paint)

SKYLIGHTS: VELUX

CEILING: wood beams (original)

INTERIOR WALLS: smooth drywall painted apricot and mango

WINDOWS/DOOR: custom cottage-style painted Swiss Coffee

FLOOR: sealed concrete (original)

BELOW: The studio "foyer" is an inviting space for informal client meetings or impromptu cocktail parties. John and Joseph have furnished the space with vintage flea-market finds. The citrus-colored upholstery and tangerine pillow livens up the seating area.

THE NEWSROOM

ABOVE: Martha and Ray transformed a 50-square-foot shed into a reporter's office with insulation, double-paned windows, and a glass-fronted door. Inside, bookshelves, a desk, and modern DSL technology make the space as efficient as a newsroom cubicle. Martha's friend Christina Glynn helped choose paint for the sunny yellow walls. They painted the original cement floor and the exterior trim blue.

OPPOSITE, FROM LEFT: In a small Santa Cruz backyard, there's room for Martha's "office," a vegetable patch, the clothesline, and a grassy play area; her daughters, Eleanor and Isabel, play here with their young cousin Jiraum. Thomas, the younger of Martha's two sons, mixes things up inside the worm bin. Raising a family, doing laundry, and growing herbs are among the many activities that keep Martha grounded in the everyday moments of life.

Working from a renovated 8-by-8-foot potting shed behind her 1937 stucco bungalow in Santa Cruz, California, Martha Mendoza doggedly pursues front-page news stories for the Associated Press. She earned the right to this unconventional arrangement after winning a Pulitzer Prize at age thirty-three.

Despite her modest environment, she is a satisfied woman. Martha jokes that working from her garden shed is a step up from her first backyard "office," which was tucked in a corner of the laundry room adjacent to the garage. "I used to look out at the old wooden garden shed, with its exposed studs and cement floor. It was filled with pots and potting soil, and I would march people over there, asking if they thought it could be an office." She enlisted Daniel Aguirre, a local carpenter, to insulate and finish the humble structure's interiors, turning it into a writer's space.

"Being detached from the house is key," says the mother of four. The laundry hangs from a clothesline stretched between the shed and bungalow. Vegetables, salad greens, strawberries, and sunflowers grow in a nearby raised bed. While Martha is on the phone, perhaps questioning a high-ranking Washington official, her daughters play on the lawn.

The paradox of this scene is one Martha sometimes finds hard to believe. "There are times when I think there's some bureaucrat in a suit whose life is about to be ruined and here I am, looking at my tomatoes."

After graduating in 1989 from UC Santa Cruz, wherever she landed, from an entry-level reporting gig for a five-thousand-circulation newspaper in central California to the *Santa Cruz Sentinel* to her first Associated Press job in New Mexico, Martha demonstrated an uncanny ability to unearth compelling and provocative stories. While covering local government, education, and business, she has exposed injustice or graft. "I've had many editors who say, 'Why don't you write nice stories?'" Martha admits. "But I'm motivated by holding people in power accountable and giving a voice to the voiceless." Martha and her husband, Ray, who has a degree in biology, moved to New York in 1997, where she joined AP's fledgling investi-

gative reporting team. She teamed with Sang-Hun Choe, a Seoul-based AP reporter, investigative researcher Randy Herschaft, and Charles Harley, a veteran special correspondent, to track down a story about the killing of South Korean civilians by American soldiers in the early days of the Korean War in 1950. The team broke the story of the incident at No Gun Ri, with a three-name byline, including Martha's.

In September 1999, the No Gun Ri story hit the wires and was published on the front pages of the *New York Times* and *Los Angeles Times*. The following spring, Martha and her colleagues won a Pulitzer Prize for investigative journalism. The team expanded on the sober account and published *The Bridge at No Gun Ri* (Henry Holt, 2001).

Hard-won, the prestige of a Pulitzer enabled her to negotiate a national investigative reporter position with AP, Martha says. "But to this day, I'm not sure any of the AP editors really understands that I'm working from a shed."

PERSONAL SPACE

NOSTALGIC FOR HER BELOVED CHILDHOOD PLAYHOUSE, MARY MARTIN GAVE NEW LIFE TO AN OLD SHED, NOW HOME TO HER MANY IMAGINATIVE VENTURES

In her updated 1930s-era "log cabin" shed, an Atlanta-based

artist and designer finds freedom to take creative risks,

whether for beekeeping or for dreaming up new products.

ABOVE: Mary salvaged a block of granite carved with the letter "M" from family property in South Carolina; it serves as the perfect doorstop. OPPOSITE: Sheltered by a canopy of shade trees at the edge of her Atlanta backyard, Mary's artful getaway takes on a welcoming glow at twilight. The property's original cabinlike structure has a newly built screened-in addition with a flagstone floor. Architecturally connected by new cedar shake roofing, landscaping, and an entry patio, the two sections give Mary distinct spaces in which to write, paint, design, and entertain.

The Life Cycle of the
Honeybee Family

Much of Mary Martin's South Carolina childhood was spent playing outside and cooking on a real stove in the pink playhouse her father, John Martin, built for her and her younger sister, Ann. "That little playhouse is a family treasure," she recalls. "We and our brother John used to have such fun parties there." Surrounded by pine trees and her mother Elizabeth's cherished camellia garden, Mary gained a love for the natural world, one that has followed her into adult life. "I remember pulling handfuls of blooms from the pale yellow Lady Banksia rose that my grandfather planted behind the playhouse and serving other children plates of petals as 'scrambled eggs,'" she laughs.

MISSION
To re-create the playhouse of her past, with a grown-up point of view

MUST-HAVES
A spacious screened-in addition with a durable stone floor, cedar shake roof, new wiring, a desk, a worktable, bookcases, and an easel

INSPIRATION
A 1950s pink playhouse, with white shutters and a Dutch door designed and built by her father for their family's Greenville, South Carolina, garden

DESIGN CHALLENGES
To connect a new screened room to a sixty-year-old asphalt-roofed shed and make the two sections relate visually to each other and the property

CREATIVE SOLUTIONS
A new cedar shake roof covers and unifies the original building and its addition. An interior doorway provides access between the 16-by-17-foot screened room and the 12-by-20-foot shed. Landscaping around both structures includes a small patio seating area, a bubbling fountain, and a shade garden to "knit" the buildings into the property.

OPPOSITE: Mary refinished the interior of the 1930s-era cabin with a fresh coat of pistachio-green paint on the board-and-batten walls and wood plank floors. Here, in one of the two original rooms, she displays beekeeping mementos on the walls and uses the work tables for designing prototypes for her latest project, Mary's Garden Champagne Savers. The sterling silver sculptures, inspired by favorite plants and flowers from Mary's borders, can be placed in a champagne bottle once opened to keep it fresh.

ABOVE LEFT: Vases and Mary's collection of vintage flower frogs are artfully displayed but are often used for creating arrangements to bring indoors. RIGHT: Partial to any shade of green, Mary found a piece of 1920s green-and-white milk glass to use for a hand-painted sign. It hangs at the entrance to her shed, beneath a carriage lantern.

OPPOSITE, LEFT: A desktop still life includes an heirloom lamp, a framed picture of Mary's childhood playhouse, a tiny four-leaf clover (Mary has a special knack for finding them), and a sterling champagne saver inspired by berries from *Cornus florida*, the flowering dogwood, from Mary's Garden collection. RIGHT: In the corner of the 1930s cabin stands an antique hutch and chair. The glow from candlesticks and wall sconces softly illuminates the room.

Fast-forward nearly forty years later: Mary still "plays" in a secreted little house tucked into the landscape behind her Southern Colonial–style home in Atlanta's historic Buckhead neighborhood. When she moved here in 1986, Mary fell in love with the humble two-room backyard structure dating to the 1930s, which has since served as her potting shed, storage for beekeeping and honey making, a painter's studio, and a writing room.

"I've never seen another one like it," she says of the 240-square-foot hut with a half-log exterior and two cottage doors. Perhaps it came here as a kit from a mail-order catalog, or maybe it was used decades ago by a gardener or children. "When I first saw it, I thought, What a wonderful place for gardening, but it has also become a nice little project building."

Mary credits her parents and grandparents for sparking her curiosity about the flowers and birds of her childhood. Her mother, Elizabeth, taught her about gardening and flower

arranging. "One of my favorite memories is of 'Mah Mah,' my grandmother, telling me, 'Sugar, pick a few leaves to go with the jonquils.' And now, all these years later, whenever I'm in my garden cutting spring flowers, I still hear her voice and smile, as I remember to pick a few leaves for the vase of narcissus, many of which came from her through my parents' garden."

Art and horticulture have followed this inventive woman throughout her life: from her first flower show at age ten, to her study of painting and drawing at the University of Georgia's School of Fine Arts, through her successful career in fashion retailing, and right up to her backyard beekeeping enterprise for producing her own wildflower honey. "Creativity and nature have been a continuous thread running through my life," she says.

Many of these endeavors—propagating plants, painting canvases, writing stories, and making camellia-blossom honey—occur inside a humble, 240-square-foot cabinlike

"I do think my childhood memories of that pink playhouse tie into my enjoyment of this very private, peaceful 'retreat' where I feel hundreds of miles away from the city when I'm inside it."

ABOVE: Mary is joined by Wallace, her cockapoo, as she serves guests afternoon champagne, cookies, and strawberries inside the screened room.

OPPOSITE, LEFT: Mary painted an ornate cast-iron gatepost in her signature green to complement the hydrangeas growing nearby. RIGHT: A curved path made with stepping stones large enough to accommodate two people walking side-by-side travels across the lawn from Mary's house to her personal backyard retreat.

OWNER Mary Martin

DESIGN

ARCHITECTURE: Kemp Mooney, Kemp Mooney Architects

ARCHITECTURAL DETAILS: David Jenkins, Continental Hardware

LANDSCAPE: David Ellis, Ellis Landesign

structure in her backyard. Reached by walking along a wide stepping-stone path that curves through the lawn to a pistachio green door, the small building is constructed from half logs and once had an asphalt-tile roof. Mary is uncertain of its provenance, but when she moved here, the shed summoned child-hood memories of her pink playhouse.

"It looked like a forgotten building, with an old roof and little landscaping," she recalls. With board-and-batten walls, double-hung windows, and cottage-style doors, it had a charm that was evident to Mary. For years, she used it for storing garden tools, growing seedlings, and starting cuttings from her roses.

In 1997, having resumed painting, she realized the shed had potential as an art studio. "I wanted to get my easel and canvases out of my house and have someplace private to paint," she recalls. The move prompted her renovation of the tiny building, including adding on a screened room. "We had a screened porch when I was a child," Mary says. "I remember all the neighborhood children gathering to play in our yard and my mother fed us straw-berries and snacks on the porch. And the family would eat together or have coffee there in the summer."

Mary asked Atlanta architect Kemp Mooney to design the screened addition and devise a way to connect it with the orig-inal shed. She showed him a photograph she took while lying on a chaise looking up at the ceiling of a Thai spirit house to illustrate the four-sided roof style she wanted. "I also showed Kemp the photo of my little playhouse," she admits.

He designed a 16-by-17-foot addition, connecting it to the shed with a new cedar shake roof and a flagstone threshold. Carriage-style lanterns almost look as if they hold flickering candles rather than lightbulbs. With exposed ceiling joists and one wall formed by the half logs of the original shed, the screened room evokes a rustic, cabinlike quality. Stacked field-stone corner sections support side walls formed by epoxy-coated aluminum screening, which doesn't rust. Mary and her guests can enjoy a glass of champagne and sweeping views of her landscape while protected from insects. "I am so happy with the way Kemp interpreted my ideas," she says.

Mary worked closely with landscape designer David Ellis to add planting beds around the structure; a profusion of camellias, mountain laurels, wild azaleas, hydrangeas, hostas, and ferns thrive here in the shade garden, softening the newness of the screened addition.

She painted a piece of 1920s milk glass creating a sign reading MARY'S GARDEN. The moniker hints at the children's rhyme, but for Mary, it symbolizes her lifelong fascination with the plant world. "To me, there has always been something natural about combining those two words—Mary and Garden," she confides. "I am always very happy out here in the garden."

MATERIALS

ROOF: cedar shake

EXTERIOR: half log (original shed); Tennessee fieldstone and epoxy-coated aluminum screening (addition)

CEILING: wood boards painted blue

INTERIOR WALLS: board and batten painted green

WINDOWS: double-hung cottage-style

DOORS: original wood painted green; vintage hardware on new screen doors

FLOORS: painted wood (shed); crab orchard flagstone (addition)

WORDPLAY

AMY BLOOM'S CHARACTER-DRIVEN NOVELS AND SHORT STORIES BEGIN WITH THE SEED OF AN IDEA THAT GROWS IN HER VIVID IMAGINATION. HERE'S WHERE AMY NURTURES AND DEVELOPS HER AWARD-WINNING WORK.

A "writing shack" just steps from the back door
is worlds away from everyday demands of
editors, publishers, and producers.

ABOVE: The sunlight dances across a stack of Amy Bloom's novels and short stories. OPPOSITE: Separate from the main residence but as comfortable as a little cottage, Amy's 14-by-14-foot writing shed is situated at the place where her cultivated backyard ends and the natural woodland begins. FOLLOWING PAGE: A trio of double-hung windows creates a glass wall offering Amy a constant perspective of nature outside. The 14-foot-long bench, made of pine, has storage cabinets and serves as an ideal work surface for organizing research or student manuscripts.

Dawn has long passed, having sent its rays streaming through the still-bare branches of early spring in New England. In the quiet of the wooded backyard, at the end of a rough-hewn flagstone path, sits a tiny house. It is silent here, but for the rustle of a few deer seeking food at the fringes of suburbia.

By late afternoon, the back door to Amy Bloom's house opens. She emerges, mug of coffee in hand, perhaps with a few folders or a spiral-bound notebook under her arm. Amy is wearing yoga pants and a hooded top with the sleeves pushed up to her elbows. She heads down the path to her shed, not hurrying, but enjoying the short journey. "It always looks to me like a bower in the woods," she says of the shaded, leafy setting.

MISSION
To devote a one-room building to the solitary act of writing

MUST-HAVES
A profusion of glass through which to view the wooded landscape; a comfortable sofa, a desk, a chair, and a lamp; bookcases and a pillow-filled window seat

INSPIRATION
A child's playhouse constructed in grown-up proportions

DESIGN CHALLENGES
To give personality to a simple box-shaped structure

CREATIVE SOLUTIONS
Amy sketched the shed and asked her carpenter-friend Roger Bryson to lend a craftsman's touch to its construction. A peaked gable over the doorway breaks up an otherwise rectangular shape. Windows on every side bring plenty of natural light into the space.

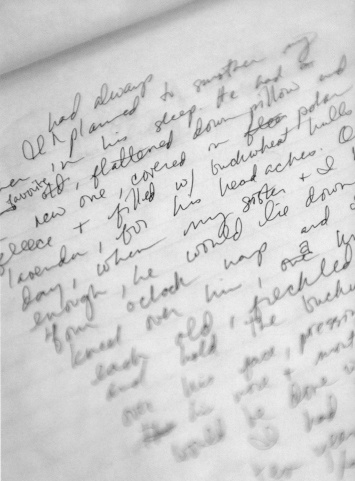

ABOVE LEFT: Interior walls and the pitched ceiling are finished with tongue-and-groove pine boards. The detailed fine carpentry encloses a triangle window at the gable's peak, offering a glimpse of the tree canopy outside. RIGHT: Amy penned several lines of a story on a yellow legal pad, one of dozens of notebooks she keeps stacked at her desk or on the window seat for moments when an idea comes to her.

Inside, propped on the desk is an embroidered sampler that reads, "There is only one joy—to love and be loved." This sentiment seems a fitting invocation for an award-winning novelist and short-story writer whose narratives explore everything from uncontrolled passion to unconditional love.

This little shed represents the intense and often solitary life of a writer, but here she is not alone. Amy's companions are the many fascinating characters that reside first in her imagination and later on the pages of her books.

When Amy moved to her 2½-acre property in southwest Connecticut in 1986, she had a full-time practice in clinical social work. She was about to begin training as an analyst when something happened to change the course of her career. In literary terms, it might be called a "plot twist," but for Amy, it was merely a story idea that overpowered her thoughts. "I remember thinking, 'I could set a murder mystery at Wesleyan University,'" she recalls, referring to the campus from her undergraduate years (she was a Phi Beta Kappa who earned a double theater–political science BA). "That's when short stories started showing up in my imagination."

Mystery writing was sidelined, though, while the complex inner world of relationships emerged as central themes of her short stories. Early encouragement from literary journals inspired Amy to write more, even while continuing to see psychotherapy clients.

"I sent off my stories to magazines and the first and second ones were selected for *Best American Short Stories* of 1991 and 1992," Amy recalls, still bemused by the unexpected inclusion of "Love Is Not a Pie" and "Silver Water" in these prestigious anthologies. She gained further acclaim for *Come to Me*, her first book of short stories named a National Book Award finalist in 1993 and as a finalist for the National Book Critics Circle Award in 2000.

A writer, therapist, lecturer at Yale, and mother, Amy wrote mostly during snatched moments, "at the kitchen table with the pale blue portable Olivetti typewriter that was my mother's," she remembers. Her oldest child, a son, was grown, but Amy's daughters were ages eight and ten when she first began writing short stories in the early 1990s. She made sure her youngest two didn't feel alienated by her literary efforts. "It was important for them to be around me, so I was very 'interruptible' then," she says. "My daughter Sarah made a sign for my door that read, 'Come in,' on one side and on the other

"The real reason my shed exists is so that I can work uninterrupted. There is no phone, no Internet in here."

BELOW: Pillows, bookcases, and familiar books—fiction, poetry, and reference volumes—are among the few items that furnish the spare interior room. There is little need for artwork on the walls, thanks to changing seasonal views of Amy's 2½-acre property outside.

OWNER
Amy Bloom

DESIGN
CONCEPT: Amy Bloom

CONTRACTOR: Roger Bryson

ABOVE: Amy worked with carpenter-friend Roger Bryson to locate the best placement for her small shed. She wanted glass-filled walls to capture an abundance of natural light. When illuminated from within, the shed's glowing presence in the woods takes on a storybook quality.

BELOW: A stained-glass "bloom" appears in the door of Amy Bloom's backyard shed.

side it said, 'Knock first, then come in.'" A fitting description of the writer's life, she acknowledges.

When her daughters were older, Amy envisioned a separate place for creativity—a little shed in the woods—and several years ago asked her friend Roger Bryson, a carpenter, to build it for her. "Roger and I went out to the woods and found the perfect spot," she explains. The site, nestled among a stand of deciduous trees, is set about 200 feet from the back door, reached via a flagstone pathway.

Its simple design, a 14-by-14-foot cedar structure with a pitched roof, gained additional charm when Amy's husband, Brian Ameche, an architect, suggested topping the front door with a peaked gable; it resembles a raised eyebrow on the structure's pleasant face.

Amy has three seating choices when she arrives to write. To the left, a tall bank of three divided windows creates a glass wall above a 14-foot-long built-in storage bench. To the right, a pine desk, formed by a long plank, holds piles of pencils, a stack of notebooks, a simple lamp, and space for a laptop. At the center, perhaps the most welcome of spots, is an oversize leather sofa, with pillows and a throw.

The rather spartan furnishings are intentional. Since the building is so well crafted, decorations are unnecessary, she says. Plus, Amy doesn't want distractions, like a telephone, the Internet, or even

photos of her children or her husband. "I just wanted a place to write on, a place to sit, and to have a lot of light," she maintains.

Amy worked here on *Away: A Novel*, published in 2007. The story about Lillian Leyb, a twenty-two-year-old Russian-Jewish immigrant to America in 1924, required extensive research, evidenced by the unusual references piled on Amy's shelves—memoirs by Alaskan trappers and gold prospectors, recordings of Yiddish singers, and maps of the Overland Telegraph Trail.

Amy's writing repertoire also includes screen-plays and teleplays. She created, wrote, and was co–executive producer for *State of Mind*, a series that debuted on the Lifetime Network in 2007, starring Lili Taylor as a psychiatrist whose life is at a crossroads.

When she leaves behind the house and its distractions for the intimate shed, Amy enjoys a soothing, somewhat ritualistic, experience. "Almost every time I go out there, I take a nap," she confides. "When I'm on the couch, I fall into a deep and instantaneous sleep. It's like my own little teleportation device."

When she wakes, often after only an hour or so, stories pour from Amy's imagination. She grabs a pad of paper or a notebook and begins writing a poignant scene, arch conversations, or a beautiful phrase.

"It's as if a little mouse writes shells of ideas there, leaving rinds of cheese strewn about for me," she says. "For me, there's always something nice about leaving the house and going to the shed. I nestle in whenever I can."

When she was young, Amy loved tree houses and playhouses, although she never had one of her own. For her, this grown-up version of a child's playhouse is satisfying. "The idea of the little house always appealed to me," she says. "I guess I love living in a big house, but I love writing in a little house."

ABOVE: A pine beam, one of two, dissects the tall ceiling overhead. Amy often takes a prewriting nap on the old leather sofa given her by a friend. When she wakes from the restorative siesta, Amy takes a seat at the plank-style desk to jot down new story ideas, an inspiring passage, or vivid dialogue.

MATERIALS

ROOF: composite roofing

EXTERIOR: beveled natural wood siding

CEILING/INTERIOR WALLS: tongue-and-groove pine boards

WINDOWS: double-hung, cottage-style

DOOR: natural pine with nine panes

FLOOR: wide-plank wood

A GARDEN GALLERY

IN A RENOVATED BOATHOUSE, A CELEBRATED PRINTMAKER CREATES COLORFUL, JOYOUS SCENES OF EVERYDAY LIFE

When her photographer-boyfriend offered Liz Lyons Friedman the use of a makeshift boathouse, she turned it into a cheery printmaking studio filled with natural light.

ABOVE: After running paper and an inked tile carving through the press, an original print called 'Wine Lovers' emerges. OPPOSITE: A 16-foot-long bank of cottage-style windows graces the southwest-facing wall of artist and printmaker Liz Lyons Friedman's studio-shed. She converted a utilitarian storage structure into a gallery for creating and displaying her fine prints. Outside the 250-square-foot building, the cactus garden reflects a passion Liz shares with her boyfriend, photographer John Gavrilis. The couple was inspired to grow their own desert landscape after numerous trips to Scottsdale art festivals.

Even as a child, Liz Lyons Friedman was an artist. Growing up in the 1950s and '60s in Buffalo, New York, she loved pencil and brush. "From the time I can remember grabbing a crayon, I always drew as a kid," she recalls. When Liz was eight years old, her first studio occupied the third-story attic of the family home. "My father hung army blankets around the space to create a little atelier for me; he used old linoleum with nursery rhymes on it for the floor," she recalls. "There was one window so I could look out over the backyard." With a rainbow of paints and a child's easel, Liz spent her summers quite contentedly, creating art in her attic nook.

MISSION
To convert a 10-by-25-foot "shoe box" that originally had three walls, one small window, and a tarp for a door into a gallerylike space for creating and displaying artwork

MUST-HAVES
A bank of windows facing the garden and ocean, plastered walls finished in a warm hue, wall-to-wall carpeting, French doors, worktables, and a printing press

INSPIRATION
An art gallery with well-lit walls and welcoming interiors

DESIGN CHALLENGES
To soften the structure's rectangular features and reflect an artist's personal style; to ensure good ventilation while using printmaking inks; to install a maximum number of windows even though one wall is backed onto a neighboring fence

CREATIVE SOLUTIONS
Liz added 16 feet of windows to the southwest-facing side of the shed, placing them high enough to accommodate her worktables underneath; she and boyfriend John Gavrilis planted a cactus garden outside the uninspiring structure and mounted a window box–like shelf so she could view potted plants at eye level

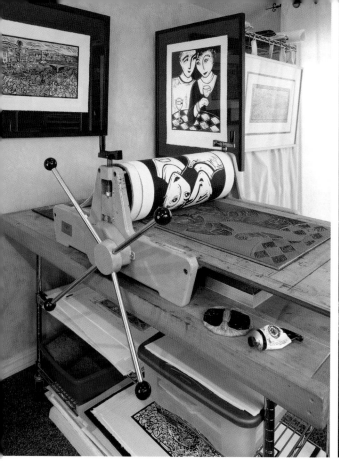

ABOVE LEFT: Liz creates prints by rolling acid-free cotton paper through her hand-cranked press. RIGHT: Once the black ink dries, Liz paints each piece of artwork with her joyful spectrum of watercolors.

PREVIOUS PAGE: Warmed by golden adobe-style plaster walls, the shed's interior is a welcoming place for artist and artwork. Liz chose carpeting with a confetti-style pattern to hide ink spills; blue-green flecks in the carpet echo the moss-colored ceiling beams overhead.

> "In designing this studio, my motive was to make it a happy space, because I make happy art."

Years later, she finds herself equally content, making linocuts in a 250-square-foot shed in Aptos, California, an art-friendly coastal community located on Monterey Bay. "I go inside and it's so peaceful there," she says. "I think back to the French ateliers, and that artists have always wanted a place to get away from everyday life and its distractions—and focus on their painting and drawing."

The teacher in Liz can't pass up an opportunity to use her artwork as a chance to educate others about printmaking. She likes to walk people through the numerous steps to create an original linoleum block print—beginning with an idea for the design, carving the linoleum block, making and finalizing test proofs, and pulling sheets of acid-free paper through her massive press, which Liz operates by hand.

She paints the final piece with vibrant watercolors, which emerge in brilliant contrast against the print's bold black lines. As a result, each work is one of a kind, in a numbered limited edition. In today's mass-produced world, Liz is an art evangelist, sharing her craft with potential customers. She meets

them in the thousands, either during the annual Santa Cruz County "Open Studios" event or at more than a dozen fine art festivals each year.

Trained as a printmaker, Liz left college with a BFA and a job teaching art at a Jesuit high school in Buffalo. The schedule allowed her to pursue an M.Ed. in art and spend her summers showing and selling her artwork at festivals and galleries. Although she "retired" in the mid-1980s, after fourteen years as a high school art teacher and three years teaching at a junior college, Liz still spends her summers on the festival circuit. She now travels to major art shows in venues like Scottsdale and Sausalito, her van packed with framed prints.

"Things have changed so much," she observes. "In the 1970s, you went out to an art and wine festival with a bunch of easels and a lawn chair. It's a business now; everything's fine-tuned and we literally build a ten-by-twenty-foot gallery for a two- to three-day show."

When Liz left her teaching position in the San Francisco Bay Area, she relocated to Sea Cliff, a hamlet on Monterey Bay.

ABOVE LEFT: Her ink-stained tools for carving linoleum blocks include those with various sizes of U- and V-shaped blades. RIGHT: Graphic black-and-white patterns appear on stacks of finished prints. Liz designates certain studio days for making matting and framing.

TOP: Liz and John bring their artistic preferences for line, form and scale to the desert garden's cactus combinations. ABOVE AND RIGHT: Liz prefers a bright watercolor palette when painting her finished prints. She often works standing at her counter-high table where she can organize and frame finished prints while also taking in views of the garden and distant ocean. The compact studio is functional and feminine, made more appealing by Liz's art-filled walls.

DESIGN
CONCEPT: Liz Lyons Friedman and John Gavrilis

Her artwork literally took over her house. "All the messy stuff was in the garage, where I had my large press and actually did the printing. Everything else was scattered throughout the house, with the drawing and carving in my office and the matting and framing occupying one of the bedrooms."

In 2001, her boyfriend, John Gavrilis, a landscape photographer who exhibits at many of the same fine art shows as Liz, offered her use of a rustic boathouse on his property in the nearby town of Aptos. "John's shed gave me an opportunity to have an art space outside my home, something I'd never before had," she says. The shoe box–like structure had "a roof, rough walls, and a canvas in front," Liz recalls.

Liz ignored the cracked concrete floor and its dim interiors, lit only by a single window. "I knew I could do something with it." Her first priority was to bring light into the room. "I decided to make it look like a cottage and add white French doors at the entrance," she explains. The doors lend charm to the rectangular building, but their presence is also pragmatic, making it easy for loading and unloading equipment and artwork. At the far end of the shed, Liz installed sliding glass doors. "Now I can open up both ends and ventilate the studio, which is important on days when I print. Having the doors open feels like I'm working outside—it's such a luxury," she says.

A 16-foot-long bank of windows, centered on the southwest wall, brings plenty of soft, natural light into the studio. "I often work standing, or sitting on a stool, so I wanted my worktables right beneath the windows." Liz textured the walls and vaulted ceiling with an adobe-style plaster and layered four colors of sunflower gold and sepia-tinged paint to create a "Tuscan" yellow room. The cheery surfaces highlight her black-framed linocuts, which are hung as if in a gallery.

The optimistic mood of Liz's studio complements *Celebrations*, the ongoing series of prints she has created for two decades. Her artwork often comes from personal experiences, such as a trip to Mexico that inspired *A Margarita with My Name on It*, or *Cooking with Wine*, a scene from John's kitchen.

Except on days when she draws, Liz's studio is a social place. "I don't often need total seclusion," she says. "People drop by to visit and John will pop in to show me what he's working on, or bring me lunch." While chatting with a customer or friend, Liz often gets out her watercolors and brushes, adding touches of lipstick red, turquoise, lime, or tangerine to sections of a linocut.

In a way, it reminds her of her childhood, when making art was for pleasure and not just for exhibiting. "When I make a piece, I hope people respond emotionally to it in a way that makes them feel good," Liz explains.

MATERIALS
ROOF: composite roofing

EXTERIOR: vertical wood siding painted gray

CEILING/INTERIOR WALLS: adobe-texture plaster faux-painted in golden hues

BEAMS: wrapped in 1-by-4-inch boards and stained green

WINDOWS: white, cottage-style, vinyl clad

DOOR: French doors; vinyl-clad sliding door

FLOOR: berber patterned, wall-to-wall carpeting

LEFT: After drawing a design onto a linoleum block, Liz uses her carving tools to cut away sections for a finished design. She was inspired to create this flower when a rare cactus bloom emerged in the garden.

REC ROOM

A YOUNG TECHNOLOGY PROFESSIONAL ADDS A BACKYARD SHED TO EXPAND AREAS FOR WORK, ENTERTAINING, AND CREATIVITY

ABOVE: An affordable alternative to building a home addition, Lin Su's 10-by-12-foot studio is ideal for her art and design projects. The interior walls are finished in maple veneer paneling. On the easel, her triptych-in-progress is titled *The Circus*.

OPPOSITE, FROM LEFT: When paired with a deck, the modular-style shed feels spacious and gives Lin's hillside property a point of view; Lin shares her landscape with "the Boss," her canine companion; created by Peter Wishinski and Zack Stratis of Los Angeles–based Ganesa Garden Design, the exotic landscape uses recycled concrete and desert plants.

By adding a 124-square-foot shed to her postage stamp–sized lot, Lin Su has more than doubled the way she enjoys and uses her urban environment. An artist who works for Yahoo's Santa Monica office as a product designer, Lin was young, single, and searching for an affordable home in Los Angeles in 2003. She also wanted enough yard space for "the Boss," her dog.

Lin graduated from the Savannah College of Art and Design in Georgia in the early 1990s. "I started off as a fine arts major, but then I changed to video and multimedia," she explains. "That's when the Internet started to manifest itself and I jumped on the bandwagon."

Her career blends a background in painting and drawing with product development and technology, but a part of her always wanted to have a design-related business. Lin factored this dream into her home search, concentrating on under-valued property with potential for a live-work arrangement.

In Los Angeles's Mount Washington neighborhood Lin purchased a 600-square-foot structure with one bedroom and one bath, probably built in the 1950s. The tiny residence was perched on a 4,900-square-foot patch of hillside overlooking Interstate 5. "It seemed to have been on the market for quite some time, probably because of how small it is," Lin says. "But it is the right amount of smallness for me."

Lin often works from home, using her living room as a remote office. A desk, computer, and monitor left little space for art projects and her painting easel. "I needed extra room to move my studio and painting out of the living room," she explains. Lin hired an architect who proposed doubling the tiny home's footprint by adding a wing for "modular" office, art, and living areas. The design included a tree house–like lookout tower to take advantage of the property's elevation and serve as Lin's studio. Its exterior featured modern proportions and materials, with horizontal lines created from wood siding, glass, and steel.

At the time, this seemed like a great solution. But Lin's budget, plus the difficulty she had finding a contractor to take on the renovations, caused her to indefinitely shelve the renovation project. She still had a space problem, though, and she found a solution at the

independent design show CA Boom, a Santa Monica exhibit featuring contemporary furniture, lighting, and architectural products.

The freestanding backyard structure designed by Ryan Grey Smith of Modern-Shed felt similar to the texture and materials her architect proposed for the now-sidelined house renovation. "It was exactly what I wanted—I could finally have the extra room I needed to move my studio out of my office."

She arranged to buy Modern-Shed's display model, which fit comfortably in the southwest corner of her property. Painted blue gray with brick red–trimmed windows and doors, the 10-by-12-foot building is oriented to capture northern light and territorial views. When the double doors are flung open, Lin enjoys the natural light painters require.

"Being in the shed makes me feel more connected—and grounded—to the creative forces that simplicity affords," Lin explains. "It's a very practical environment that offers a great escape from all the complexities that surround me."

ART
AND SOUL

RESTING MIDWAY BETWEEN SUNNI RUDD'S HOUSE AND A SHADY RAVINE, A WISTFUL GARDEN SHED INSPIRES CREATIVITY AS SHE DOODLES AND DRAWS FAVORITE BLOSSOMS FOR HER GREETING-CARD LINE

Built from one-hundred-year-old materials and decorated
with Depression glass and timeworn furniture, Sunni Rudd's shed
resembles a well-preserved structure from the past.

ABOVE: Weather-beaten but full of character, a collection of birdhouses mounted on posts dots the Rudd landscape. OPPOSITE: Recycled barn wood, vintage windows, and historic architectural details give Sunni Rudd's shed a patina of age. Sunni hung Battenberg lace curtains in the windows and planted a cottage-style perennial and herb garden around its perimeter. A hand-painted sign over the tiny porch reads SUNNI'S GARDEN SHED. FOLLOWING PAGE: Sunni uses her potting bench for everything from growing herb cuttings to sketching her botanical greeting cards.

"Here's where I keep everything I want to save and love. This is my little comfort zone, my quiet place."

—SUNNI RUDD

Sunni Rudd, a greeting-card illustrator and avid gardener, envisioned a potting shed for her half-acre Seattle garden. Like her quirky handmade drawings of flowers, hearts, hands, and symbols, though, she imagined a structure that was beyond everyday expectations. "I always thought I needed a shed, but I held off for years because I didn't want something from a hardware store," Sunni says. "I wanted a shed with character, like an enlarged playhouse."

MISSION
To erect a character-infused and farm-inspired building in a once-neglected spot in the landscape where its owner comes to think, read, draw, and garden

MUST-HAVES
A covered porch, "a whole bunch of little windows," salvaged shutters, a vintage screen door, a metal roof, a potting bench, and a daybed

INSPIRATION
A rustic barn retrofitted for a city landscape

DESIGN CHALLENGES
Accessing and building a level structure on a long, narrow slice of land that gradually slopes from the sidewalk to a protected creek

CREATIVE SOLUTIONS
Builder Norm Steelhammer constructed the walls (windows and door included) off-site and delivered the shed in pieces, ready for assembly. Joel Rudd built a level platform as its base, a "floor" on pier blocks. Sunni planted a perennial garden to hide the under-pinnings of the exposed posts.

Like her lifelong nickname, Sunni is an exuberant person, the type who even into her fifth decade continues to draw a little star over the "i" when she signs her name. She has an optimist's knack for turning small gifts into grand gestures that nurture those around her. For example, in 1985, when Sunni and her husband found a 1,200-square-foot postwar bungalow in south Seattle, she wasn't daunted by its two tiny bedrooms and single bath. Instead she turned it into a Victorian-inspired cottage, painting it light pink and adding soft green shutters and a gingerbread-style roof.

The Rudds' lot is sizable by urban standards. But the one-third acre of land is configured as a 60-by-360-foot slice, gradually descending to a protected greenbelt at the edge of Taylor Creek. Sunni and Joel coped with the challenges of gardening here by cutting several terraces into the verdant but hilly property.

The idea of a garden shed emerged ten years ago when Sunni's artwork and gardening projects outgrew their small home. She first considered a greenhouse, but wanted a space that accommodated more than housing tender plants. "I needed a place where I could leave things out and they wouldn't

be in anybody else's way," she explains. She convinced Joel, a sales executive, that the garden's middle "terrace" would be an ideal place for a structure. "I knew I wanted it on the side of the yard so it would get southern sun. But I didn't want something that was 'just a shed.' It needed to look like it was original to the property," Sunni explains.

After seeing several sheds Norm Steelhammer created from salvaged barn wood, Sunni commissioned the Centralia, Washington, farmer to build one for her. She adhered to his standard size—10 by 20 feet—but requested special elements like vintage windows, a 5-foot-deep covered porch, and a tin roof. "I wanted the porch so I could have my coffee and enjoy Seattle's rain without getting soaked," she says. "You can hear the rain fall onto the corrugated metal roof, which is the most soothing sound to me."

The Rudds used a dose of ingenuity to figure out how to erect the 200-square-foot structure halfway down a sloping yard, especially one with no alley or driveway access. Joel built a platform to serve as its base, staggering the pier block–mounted posts to create a level floor. Steelhammer constructed each wall

ABOVE LEFT: A quilt-covered chaise entices Sunni to spend time catching up on reading seed catalogues or taking an afternoon nap. RIGHT: Sunni displays her Depression glass and vintage tool collections in a primitive canning shelf. She makes room between vases, bowls, and pitchers to tuck Mason jars filled with seeds and pods collected from her garden.

ARCHITECTURE:
Norm Steelhammer,
Sunni Rudd

CONSTRUCTION:
Norm Steelhammer,
Joel Rudd

INTERIOR DESIGN: Sunni
Rudd

LANDSCAPE DESIGN:
Sunni Rudd

ABOVE: Battenberg lace curtains carry the charm of Sunni's Victorian-style residence outdoors to her garden shed.

TOP LEFT: Sunni's cutting garden yields country-style blooms, including a mixed arrangement of dahlias displayed against a blue garage door. RIGHT: Vintage windows, lace curtains, and garden collectibles enhance the interior setting.

and the roof separately at his shop 75 miles away before trucking it to Seattle. "We dragged all the pieces down to the site and spent seven hours bolting the shed together," Sunni recalls.

Unfinished studs display glassware, framed pictures, and art supplies. A vintage canning shelf, its blue-green paint chipping away with age, contains vases, flowerpots, and seed-filled jars. Sunni laughingly remembers Joel's offer to sand and repaint the old cupboard: "He wants to fix everything up, and I want it to stay rustic."

The garden shed's presence in Sunni's life inspires her many artistic endeavors, including Aunt Coco's Cottage, a Web-based gift and greeting-card venture she launched in 2004. Sunni created the business to market a line of beautifully packaged "message in a bottle" gifts. But she began to draw playful flower portraits while recovering from her third surgery to repair a recurring shoulder injury. "I just started drawing the flowers that I was longing to be planting out in my garden." With her good arm Sunni sketched a bouquet of blooms—a poppy, a lupine, a foxglove, a delphinium, and other flowers— and hand-colored each with a palette of bright and pastel hues.

Today there are nearly a dozen lines of her popular Aunt Coco's Cottage note cards, expanded to include more flowers,

MATERIALS

ROOF: Galvanized tin

SKYLIGHTS: Tongue-and-groove horizontal siding recycled from a century-old Washington barn, painted red

INTERIOR WALLS: Exposed studs, unpainted

FLOOR: Vinyl sheeting, confetti pattern

WINDOWS: Salvaged cottage windows, painted white

DOOR: Vintage cottage door (white) and screen door (dark green), original paint allowed to chip

plus hands, hearts, and graphic symbols. And like her mirthful nickname, Sunni says drawing each one has given her a way to express happiness in a difficult situation.

Whatever her mood, Sunni experiences newfound joy when she escapes the pace of the everyday and retires to her garden shed. Perhaps she'll doodle at the counter, gazing outside at a favorite perennial worthy of capturing on paper. Or she will start a flat of flowers, using seeds collected the previous fall. While lounging on the quilt-covered daybed with a journal in her lap, Sunni might even take a short siesta. "I have a hard time slowing down," she confides. "But when I come here I want the solitude of my garden shed. It keeps me on an even keel. It keeps me planted."

ABOVE: The shed's exterior, made from one-hundred-year-old salvaged barn wood is a place to display garden artwork, including this collection of "sunny" plaques, in honor of Sunni's lifelong nickname. TOP: Sunset-hued dahlias fill a bumbleblee-shaped container that Sunni hangs on the salvaged door's cut-glass knob.

A PLACE FOR PLANTS AND PLANT LOVERS

"I always wanted to find a place in the country—a retreat. And for years, I had plans for this potting shed in my mind."

—SYLVIA WILLIAMS

Part function and part folly, the best potting shed is centrally placed in a well-designed landscape. In spring and summer, gardeners use their sheds for starting herbs and flowers on the windowsill. In autumn, they fill the shelves and benches with tender plants requiring shelter from the elements.

By winter, you'll find a gardener curled up in a sunny window of her "nest," browsing through seed catalogues or filling the pages of a journal with next year's planting scheme. Clever design and high comfort combine to make these settings perfect for both horticultural and garden parties (because once you have a fanciful garden shed, you'll want to share it with fellow plant lovers).

Architecturally, potting places echo features of the main residence. They serve as a vertical element upon which vines may climb and garden ornamentation or vintage tools are displayed. A garden shed reflects the creativity of those who find their most pleasurable moments with their hands in the soil.

SUNCATCHER

A GLASS-AND-CEDAR GREENHOUSE SHELTERS TENDER PLANTS, CHERISHED COLLECTIONS, AND TREASURED FRIENDS

In the heart of Washington State's apple country,

an art collector and an antiques dealer

create a winsome and welcoming garden haven.

Michelle and Rob Wyles have quietly acquired an extraordinary collection of early-American folk sculpture. While Rob is taken with nineteenth- and early-twentieth-century carved figures—cigar store Indians, carousel animals, trade signs, and life-size characters—Michelle is drawn to 1930s pottery and garden ornamentation. This penchant for authentic Americana and humble, utilitarian items imbues the design for their 20-by-20-foot greenhouse. With four gables, a set of stained-glass panels, and Gothic windows, it is the centerpiece of what Michelle describes as her "farmer's wife's vegetable garden."

MISSION
To design an eclectic sanctuary in the sun

MUST-HAVES
"Room for a party," plus spacious windows, flooring from native Cascade mountain rock, ample display shelves for a pottery collection, and running water

INSPIRATION
An uncomplicated Nantucket-style cottage finished in weathered shingles and lavender trim

DESIGN CHALLENGE
To emulate a greenhouse's best features (light, air circulation, humidity control) without mimicking its structure

CREATIVE SOLUTIONS
A quartet of symmetrically placed gables and four window-filled walls flood the interior with light. Salvaged windows and French doors produce a glass-walled design. Hinged panels open to encourage air flow; a ceiling fan circulates air. A layer of crushed gravel beneath interior shelves disperses humidity in summer.

"The idea of having a party in a greenhouse is intimate and romantic. It puts people in close proximity to the things we love."

—MICHELLE WYLES

ABOVE: Instead of windows, one section of the west-facing wall accommodates the antique cupboard that holds some of Michelle's celadon, turquoise, mint, and jade-colored pieces of McCoy pottery. Originally considered affordable everyday dishware, the 1920s, '30s, and '40s urns, bowls, vases, jugs, and flower-pots are highly collectible. Filled with glass floats, a pair of white antique cast-iron planters rests on the counter, between which is one of Michelle's favorite begonias.

ABOVE LEFT: Elevated on a post above the garden, a cluster of wooden birdhouses has been weathered by eastern Washington's hot, dry summers and chilly winters. Growing beneath the birdhouses is a rugged agave.
RIGHT: "When you live out in the country, you have to entertain yourself," Michelle maintains. She installed a 1940s kitchen sink to bring hot and cold water into the green house. Mounted on a stainless-steel counter, the sink is ideal for gardening projects, such as arranging bouquets of flowers cut from the garden.

Whether you call it a glass house or a summer cottage, the shed situated at the far edge of Michelle and Rob's Yakima Valley garden was created as a peace offering of sorts. It replaced an ordinary plastic greenhouse where Michelle, an accomplished Master Gardener, started tomato seedlings and wintered tender perennials. Surrounded by raised vegetable beds, the prefab structure "functioned very well in this spot for eight years," Michelle maintains.

But by 2004, Rob's expanding collection of American folk sculpture had grown, migrating to their home's house plant–filled solarium next to the kitchen. "Adding a greenhouse in the garden was Rob's way of bribing me when he kicked me out of the solarium," Michelle jokes. "He told me I could build whatever I wanted out there."

Michelle seized the chance to create her dream "greenhouse": an artful structure to contain hothouse plants and collections of pottery and antiques, where she could install vintage windows and architectural fragments that she had stockpiled over the years. As an antiques dealer and owner of Garden Dance, a local shop, Michelle describes herself as someone who has "an affinity for weird things that have no

particular function." Rob, her husband of thirty years, agrees that Michelle is attracted to quirky treasures, but maintains that his wife has "a good eye for design."

She first sketched a window-filled structure, then added an attractive four-gabled roofline. "I'm partial to square buildings. I added shingled siding, which reminds me of homes I'd seen while vacationing in Nantucket years ago." She left the cedar unstained and used lavender paint on the windows, doors, and trims, explaining, "It's a happy color."

The building's abundance of glass invites sunshine during eastern Washington's winters, when temperatures dip into the low teens. Two Gothic windows, which Rob and Michelle hauled home from Hayden, Idaho, create architectural interest on the side walls; they are bracketed by fifteen-pane French doors serving as windows. More Gothic millwork appears above the doorway and vintage stained glass is mounted at the peaks of two gables.

The design process was anything but logical, Michelle admits. "You can be unrealistic and impractical when you're making a garden building. The beauty of this one is the juxta-position of its fanciness with its humility. It's not supposed to

ABOVE LEFT: The walls and shelving inside the greenhouse are made from unstained plywood boards. Here, a low shelf can serve as either a window seat or a display shelf (there is storage beneath for watering cans and flowerpots). Rob added the turn-of-the-twentieth-century cast-stone lamb to his collection after falling for its humble simplicity. "To me, it is just a beautiful piece that is very minimal but also spiritual. I wonder, What was the person thinking when he made it?" RIGHT: The tray hanging from an early twentieth-century scale doubles as a plant stand. A sunflower bouquet is arranged in a piece from Michelle's collection of green McCoy pottery.

OWNERS
Michelle and Rob Wyles

DESIGN
ARCHITECTURE/INTERIOR: Michelle Wyles, Garden Dance

CONTRACTOR/BUILDER: Gale Curtis

LANDSCAPE: Michelle Wyles

"Look through the hedge and there's a hint of something inside, but you're surprised to see the greenhouse—it's not what you'd expect."

—ROB WYLES

be a la-di-da building, but it is a manifestation of things that make me happy."

Michelle finds it hard to pinpoint a single design influence. "Although I don't consider myself an artist, my mother was an artist and I seem to surround myself with artists, so I guess the inspiration rubs off. Artists use their experiences plus everything they've ever read or seen or heard about to come up with ideas. My choice of this style of greenhouse was more than likely just serendipity."

Come summer, the doors and windows are flung open to infuse the garden house with the fragrances of roses and herbs such as lavender. Rob and Michelle host parties here for friends or to benefit charities like the Yakima Area Arboretum, their local public garden. It may be dark outside, but when the stars above are shining, the music is playing, and up to ten revelers are gathered around the large round table, it's a magical scene for Rob: "People and plants are in their glory—to me, that's the fun of being out here."

OPPOSITE, FROM LEFT: Mint-condition McCoy cachepots and an antique iron birdbath supported by a nymph create a dining table still life; illuminated at dusk, the glowing interior highlights a Gothic window at the gabled roofline's peak; brick that Michelle salvaged from an old school building forms a basket-weave pathway around the shed's perimeter. ABOVE: Michelle grows roses, lavender, and many perennials for her flower arrangements. RIGHT: The expansive blue skies of Eastern Washington offer brilliant contrast to the natural cedar-clad greenhouse.

MATERIALS
ROOF: cedar shingles

EXTERIOR: cedar shingles

SKYLIGHTS: VELUX

INTERIOR WALLS: sealed plywood sheeting

WINDOWS/DOOR: architectural salvage

FLOOR/FOUNDATION WALLS: Cascades basalt rubble

SUBURBAN FOLLIES

POPULATED BY A FANCIFUL SHED, A CHICKEN COOP, A VIEWING TOWER, AND A PLAYHOUSE, A GARDEN VILLAGE COMES TO LIFE

When a passionate plantswoman
and a relentless builder turn their attention
to the garden, fantasy rules.

ABOVE: A collector of chicken and egg paraphernalia, Kathy Fries displays this cast-iron trio on a bed of sedge planted in a tree stump. OPPOSITE: The Palais des Poulets (also known as "Clucking Hen Palace") was transformed from a decrepit shed into a functional and decorative chicken coop. Clematis entwines a vintage ironwork fence and scrambles up the capricious-looking turret. PAGE 71: Like the EGGS sign shown opposite, Kathy has a penchant for old poultry farm implements, including this assemblage of watering cans, feed bags, and vintage hen figures.

Kathy and Ed Fries acquired their 1.3-acre property in 1992. They overlooked the quirky 1960s beach house, bramble-covered land, and two crumbling sheds because of the uninterrupted views of Mount Rainier and 90 feet of private beachfront on Lake Washington. Priorities changed when Kathy, who worked for an aerospace firm, planted sunflowers and scarlet runner beans in a vegetable patch abandoned by the prior owners. "I had that childlike experience of amazement at having grown something and kept it alive," she recalls. "I just felt so accomplished."

MISSION
To transform a long, narrow, dark strip of land into a wooded wonderland colonized by useful—and enchanting—garden structures

MUST-HAVES
Each of the four sheds plays a role in Kathy's garden design narrative. Whether it houses exotic poultry, provides a blissful outlook, gathers garden friends, or invites play, Kathy's structures feature artful details and pleasing finishes.

INSPIRATION
Kathy envisioned a magical landscape where young and old experience the innocent wonder of nature and its flora and fauna. "I want those who come here to be a part of the whimsy and remember their own childhoods," she says.

DESIGN CHALLENGES
The property measures 880 feet long and as narrow as 50 feet in some spots. An asphalt driveway intersects the length of the lot. Two storage sheds, their openings covered in plastic tarp, were prominent eyesores.

CREATIVE SOLUTIONS
Collaborating with Seattle builder and artist John Akers, Kathy has transformed the ramshackle sheds into eye-pleasing garden buildings. One, now called the Palais des Poulets, is home to the chicken coop, while another, which mimics Venice's Doge's Palace, is large enough for preschool birthday parties or horticultural society workshops.

<blockquote>
I'd give all the wealth that years have piled / The slow result of life's decay / To be once more a little child / For one bright summer day.

—LEWIS CARROLL, "SOLITUDE"
</blockquote>

A few lines in a 1856 Lewis Carroll poem express Kathy's vision for her garden. Even if she weren't a mother of two young boys, it was inevitable that this former aerospace project manager, now a horticulturist and a naturalist, would draw from favorite childhood summers as the inspiration for her landscape.

Kathy and her husband, Ed Fries, who spearheaded Microsoft's Xbox launch in 2000 and is now a game design consultant, have spent fifteen years transforming this slender wedge of land on the shore of Seattle's Lake Washington into a verdant wonderland. Because their two-bedroom 1960s beach house is small, Kathy considers the garden—and its buildings—as an extension of the family's living space.

The property's limitations are overlooked by anyone who journeys past collections of shade-loving plants, including rhododendrons, rare ferns, hostas, epimediums, trilliums, arisaemas, and terrestrial orchids, which together form a delicate tapestry on the woodland floor. Active in the Seattle horticultural community, Kathy frequently hosts garden tours and workshops here.

With eyes glued to the margins of the paths, in search of yet another unusual perennial or groundcover, visitors are suddenly interrupted by a cluster of unlikely buildings occupying the garden. To call them "sheds" is a bit of an understatement; these are artful installations. Truly, the only word to describe them is "folly." One architectural dictionary says a folly is an extravagant structure built as a conversation piece or a sculptural element in the landscape, typically without any functional purpose. In Kathy's mind, however, function and beauty should coexist. The trio of garden follies, along with a child-size playhouse used by her sons, dots the landscape and serves as a backdrop to her ever-expanding plant collections.

The first structure Kathy created was something this Minnesota native had always wanted: part potting shed and

BELOW, FROM LEFT: Five-year-old Xander enjoys helping his mom gather eggs from the nests for breakfast; two-year-old Jasper plays inside the kid-size shed, also built by John Akers from recycled barn wood; the side of the chicken coop serves as an ideal backdrop for a collection of antique signage letters that spell out Ed's and Kathy's names.

OPPOSITE, LEFT: Kathy and carpenter John Akers created a trowel-and-tool "clock" as a way to display timeworn garden gizmos. RIGHT: Tucked into one corner of the coop is a salvaged cast-iron sink and ledges filled with more chicken finds.

TOP: Ornate iron hardware and a cut-glass knob add Victorian elegance to the salvaged chicken coop door.

part chicken coop. She enlisted John Akers, a Seattle craftsman who works with salvaged and recycled materials, to rebuild a tarp-covered lean-to.

Akers sketched a 10-by-16 foot building, complete with turret, cupola, and leaded windows. Kathy ordered vintage knobs and hinges from eBay and quizzed local feed stores to determine specifications for the coops and nests.

As a finishing touch, Kathy personalized the rustic structure with a collection of antique sign letters that spell out ED & KATHY FRIES in a hodgepodge of colors and fonts.

Kathy next collaborated with Akers to erect a 26-foot-tall tower to elevate a diminutive, octagonal, 6-by-7-foot Gothic-style shed. He originally built the structure for a display garden at the Northwest Flower and Garden Show in Seattle. "He called to see if I wanted to buy it when the show was over," Kathy says. "I told him, 'Only if you can make it into a tower so I can view my knot garden.'"

To lift the building, Akers constructed a 12-foot-high platform with steps and an iron railing. It's well worth the climb up a narrow staircase to reach the tower: the French doors are thrown open and visitors lean over the iron railing and admire the medieval-inspired knot garden below.

Kathy and Ed were thrilled with their stylish coop—potting shed and elegant viewing tower, but an ugly flat-roofed doorless shack that stood halfway down the driveway nagged at them. The 20-by-20-foot structure with aluminum siding and a slanting dirt floor stored tools, a lawn mower, a leaf shredder, and garden hoses. Kathy would rush visitors past it, distracting them by pointing to an unusual Japanese hydrangea in the distance.

"Anybody else would have mowed the whole thing down fifteen years ago," Kathy acknowledges. "But our philosophy has been to use what we have and make it work, rather than just destroy it. I had an idea of creating a multifunction garden building that's also a beautiful garden element."

After showing Kathy a book about Venetian architecture, Akers suggested that they retrofit the shack and style it as a miniature Doge's Palace. "John had the idea of re-creating a

European village, where there are multiple follies, and suddenly it makes the whole garden work," Kathy says.

Gardener Alejandro Gamundi leveled the dirt foundation and worked with Akers to install a plywood floor. The men replaced the structure's south wall and a section of the roof with corrugated greenhouse panels, bringing light inside for both people and plants. An 18-foot-tall corner clock tower and arched millwork break up the building's boxy shape. Akers proudly calls the building "outrageous" and says it is the finishing touch to the landscape: "Now there's the feeling of an Italian town square, when you see the buildings clustered together."

Kathy and Ed realize that their house is too small for a family of four, but with its enviable waterfront location, moving is out of the question. The Doge's Palace can handle everything from preschool parties to plant-propagation classes to storage. "People don't necessarily need more *house* as much as they need more *places* to be where they can have fun and utilize their outdoor spaces," Kathy says.

ABOVE LEFT: "This tower is my attempt to give a viewpoint to the knot garden, and to catch glimpses of the sailboats on the lake beyond our property," Kathy says. The octagonal tower rests on a 12-foot-tall platform with steps and an iron railing. A copper roof, topped with a domed turret, gives the structure a grand presence among a canopy of Douglas firs, madronas, and western red cedars. RIGHT: After helping Kathy and Ed create their many follies, John Akers suggested a fitting solution for the property's ugly 20-by-20-foot aluminum shed. He turned it into a Doge's Palace–inspired garden house and embellished the façade with verdigris copper sheeting and Kathy's assortment of vintage medallions, hardware, and figures (see page 74).

PLANTING PARADISE

FUNCTIONAL AND ATTRACTIVE, A TIDY GARDEN SHED IS THIS LANDSCAPE'S ORNAMENTAL AND ARCHITECTURAL FOCAL POINT

When she takes a break from corporate demands, Joan Enticknap makes a beeline for her garden. The potting shed is at its heart, where she happily whiles away her weekend hours.

ABOVE: Bank president by day, Joan Enticknap is a contented weekend horticulturist. OPPOSITE: Designed for both practicality and charm Joan's potting shed is finished with cedar shingles. She chose a taupe paint that has purple undertones, matching the shingles on her home. The attractive standing-seam copper roof is topped with a finial and louvered vents. Fragrant lavender grows close to the entrance, requiring Joan to brush against it, which releases its heady aromas as she works in the garden.

Britain's horticultural obsession was evident to Joan Enticknap on a trip to visit relatives in England. She observed owners of humble vegetable patches and stately country gardens tending with great care to their plants and borders. The potting shed—a ubiquitous feature of English gardens—captured her imagination. "No matter what size a garden was, it had some kind of garden shed," she says. "Even little row houses with tiny backyards found room for one." Joan loved the way these small buildings defined and lent character to gardens. "The English have incorporated potting sheds charmingly as part of their landscapes—and I thought, Some day, I'm going to have a garden shed, too."

MISSION
To build a working shed for storing vintage and modern-day tools, seeds, and flowerpots

MUST-HAVES
Shelves and hooks for storage, a potting bench, running water, operable windows, double French doors wide enough to accommodate a wheelbarrow, and a finial-topped cupola

INSPIRATION
Joan admired the four distinctive, octagonal garden houses at Mount Vernon, George and Martha Washington's Virginia home. Said to be used for storing seeds and tools, the structures were both practical and decorative.

DESIGN CHALLENGES
To blend two motivating inspirations—the function of an English potting shed and the character of early-American garden houses

at Washington's Mount Vernon

CREATIVE SOLUTIONS
Joan worked with Seattle architect Gregory Bader to adapt the design so it complemented her 1914 Arts and Crafts house. They decided on an almost square 8-by-9-foot shed with chamfered corners. "We softened the effect of a boxy shape," Bader explains. A cupola and finial add finishing touches to the copper roof.

ABOVE LEFT: The near view toward Joan's garden is filled with an explosion of *Lavandula* x *intermedia* 'Provence', a haven for bees. The climbing rose and clematis-clad arbor appears in the distance, across a strolling lawn. RIGHT: In their simplicity, Joan's vintage hose nozzles reveal a utilitarian beauty. Thanks to frequent contributions from her brother, her growing collection symbolizes Joan's childhood in an agricultural community and her present-day love of gardening.

PREVIOUS PAGE: As comfortable as a Karl Larson painting, the shed's buttery yellow interior is both practical and beautiful. Joan's potting bench displays terra-cotta pots, vintage hose nozzles, and a weathered watering can. A pair of small mullioned windows swings open on hinges.

Within Joan's banker persona resides the right-brained point of view of an artist. The president and chief operating officer of Seattle-based HomeStreet Bank, Joan chaired Washington State's public facilities district during the development of Safeco Field, home to Major League Baseball's Seattle Mariners. She calls herself the "design conscience of the ballpark," which has been recognized as one of the country's top 150 buildings by the American Institute of Architects. Joan believes that the quality of materials and workmanship determines the strength of a project's design. "For example, I became obsessed with getting the right color of green at the ballpark—one that works in our gray Northwest weather," she says. "If I see a new ballpark sign that's painted the wrong green, I'm the first to call and have it changed."

"If I'm inside my shed and it's raining outside, I feel cozy. On warm days, I pull my chair out to the shed, open the windows and doors, and enjoy the view of my garden."

When she leaves the office and ball field behind, Joan gravitates to her garden, a 100-by-125-foot lot in a historic Seattle neighborhood. Surrounded by climbing and shrub roses, lavender and germander, a perennial cutting garden, and heirloom vegetable beds, Joan finds contentment in the simple tasks of pruning, planting, and weeding. "I grew up on twenty acres outside Seattle and we all gardened—canning and freezing everything we grew. My siblings and I all vowed never to have a garden as adults," she confides. Happily, she's traveled full circle from her youth, as Joan now willingly grows beans, tomatoes, baby pumpkins, cucumbers, plums, and vibrant dahlias in raised beds adjacent to her potting shed.

Joan loves English-style gardens but turned to a purely American source for the design of her garden shed. "I've been to Mount Vernon at least four times," she says. "Every time I travel east, I visit. I love the octagonal shape of its seed and tool houses. Just looking at them makes me happy." Joan asked architect Gregory Bader to create a potting shed that complemented her 1914 two-story brick-and-cedar-shingle home.

"I wanted materials that matched my house—shingles and

ABOVE LEFT: Mounted on an exposed stud, a reproduction oak leaf bracket holds Joan's oft-used tools. RIGHT: Classic cottage garden flowers, these dahlias grow in raised beds adjacent to the potting shed. A popular Northwest crop, dahlias thrive in this landscape, offering their long-blooming stems for Joan's cut arrangements.

LEFT: The arbor provides an inviting passage for those approaching the formal lawn. A diamond-patterned bluestone walk leads the eye towards the perfectly-proportioned potting shed.

OPPOSITE, LEFT: A stand of white coneflowers (*Echinacea purpurea* 'Alba') punctuates the border with graphic petals. RIGHT: Cottage-style windows and wood trim are finished in a lighter shade of the shed's chocolate-taupe paint color.

a brick base," she points out. She placed newspaper ads to buy recycled clinker bricks and drove around Seattle's older areas looking for just the right paint color to draw out the bricks' plum shade. The resulting custom paint is a chocolate taupe with purple undertones.

Inside, the shed's exposed wall studs provide "nooks and crannies" for displaying Joan's collection of vintage garden hose nozzles (she has more than one hundred), many of them found at garage sales and flea markets by her brother, Steven.

The small shed has ample storage and is fitted with hinged cottage windows and a pair of double French doors. "The cut-off corners of the octagonal shape also gave me spaces for shelves—I can stack my pots and tools there. And the wall hooks preserve floor space," she points out.

When the doors are thrown open, a warm, yellow interior is revealed. "I chose the 'Provençal' yellow as a contrast to Seattle's gray days," Joan explains, again displaying her savvy color sensibility. "If I'm inside my shed and it's raining outside, I feel cozy. On warm days, I pull my chair out to the shed, open the windows and doors, and enjoy the view of my garden."

OWNER
Joan Enticknap

DESIGN
ARCHITECTURE: Gregory Bader, Bader Architecture

CONTRACTOR: Mike Adams, Adams Construction Services

LANDSCAPE: Tom Zachary and Francine Day, Tom Zachary Landscape Architects

Landscape architects Tom Zachary and Francine Day translated Joan's memories of her favorite English gardens into a design that includes a welcoming arbor, a formal strolling lawn, a sunken white garden, and a knot garden planted with herbs. A bluestone path, laid on the east-west axis, draws visitors beneath a 15-foot-long arbor and into the garden. Swathed in four climbing roses and two clematis vines, the cedar arbor frames a view of the copper-roofed potting shed, an attractive focal point in the distance.

Joan says that her very mood changes as she walks beneath this fragrant tunnel. "There's an arrival sequence in this garden. As you peer beyond the arbor, you're pleased and surprised to discover the potting shed. It's designed to be looked at and enjoyed."

"As you peer beyond the arbor, you're pleased and surprised to discover the potting shed. It's designed to be looked at and enjoyed."

HAMPTON HUT

A GRAND SCULPTURE GARDEN GAINS A MARITIME-INSPIRED TOOLSHED FOR STORING THE WHEELBARROW AND WATERING CANS

Characteristic of historic fishing huts that dot the shores of

Long Island's North Fork, John Barham's shed is

worthy of its eighteenth-century roots.

ABOVE: Blackened hardware, inspired by a centuries-old heart motif, appears on the hinged door of John Barham's tool shed. OPPOSITE: Primitive shelving displays a birdhouse collection alongside the shed's exterior. FOLLOWING PAGE: The entry porch has a herringbone-pattern brick floor and carved columns. John replicated the white column (with nesting holes for birds) from an eighteenth-century fisherman's house. The twin boards from Turkey, embedded with sharp stones, are used to thrash wheat.

John Barham often passed a small weathered house on Long Island's North Fork. Like many buildings from the turn of the nineteenth century, it had shingles turned silvery gray from exposure to saltwater and other elements. The white-trimmed windows and sturdy doors with wrought-iron hardware not only revealed East Coast pragmatism but also evoked a humble charm. Hinged barn doors opened to accommodate a boat, while white shutters flanked the windows.

John stopped to talk with the elderly fisherman who owned the house to ask permission to take exact measurements of it. He thought it would be the ideal structure for a garden shed to fit into the new landscape he and his late partner, Richard "Dick" Auer, were developing in Bridgehampton.

MISSION
To reproduce a tiny house with timeless charm to adorn a 2-acre garden and store fertilizer, flowerpots, glass cloches, and vintage garden tools

MUST-HAVES
A double door with low ramp for wheelbarrow and lawn mower access, double-hung windows with shutters, a cupola with an antique weather vane, storage shelves, and electricity

INSPIRATION
A nostalgic one-room structure inhabited by a seasoned fisherman, his wife, and a boat

DESIGN CHALLENGES
To reproduce a building he admired from afar, having never seen its interior

CREATIVE SOLUTIONS
With the owner's permission, John took precise measurements of the building's exterior, including placement of windows and doors, its roof angle, and its height. He designed the interior to fit his garden storage needs, adapting what was originally a very small house into a working shed.

ABOVE LEFT: A classic bust perched at the window ledge of John's garden shed overlooks the garden. Overhead are hooks from which hang rusted fishing implements, their usefulness long since abandoned although they are beautiful to observe. RIGHT: Magnetic bars provide John with the perfect storage solution for a metal scythe, ax, saw, clippers, and other implements (including two ancient horseshoes).

Reproduced board for board, the tiny structure sits in the northwest corner of John's elegant landscape. It serves a useful purpose but also reflects Long Island's seafaring history. John never saw the original building's interior and it has since collapsed, but his imagination conjures up a great romance between fisherman and wife. "They must have really loved each other to live for so long in that small place," he muses.

If he were to describe a motivating theme for his life, John might use the phrase "a grand passion." From a young age, he has been beguiled by the natural world. "Gardening is the greatest pleasure in my life," he says. "It's more than pleasure, it's a religion; it's part of my soul." John's affection for plants began nearly eighty years ago when he was six. He credits his cousin Roland Totten, after whom the University of North Carolina at Chapel Hill's botany department is named, with teaching him how to identify and name southern plants like wild irises and orchids. "Roland instilled in me a love of gardening," John recalls. "All of the positive moments of my life occurred with plants and the garden."

As a young man returning from a stint flying B17s and B29s for the Air Corps, John moved to New York City to attend the Parsons School of Design. He later studied painting and design at Académie Julien in Paris and the American Academy in Rome, experiences that forever influenced his aesthetic sensibility.

Wherever he lived, John always managed to create a garden. He fondly recalls filling a balcony with flowers and shrubs at his Fifty-seventh Street apartment in New York (delighting his neighbor Gypsy Rose Lee), and planting a tiny courtyard with flowers just steps from the Eiffel Tower in postwar Paris. In the 1950s he lived on Perry Street in the West Village and worked as a decorator at Lord & Taylor. His tiny garden there became the setting for Thursday-night cocktail parties, famous among his friends.

By the late 1970s, John divided his time between San Francisco and the Hamptons, where he rented the same cottage each summer. He acquired an undeveloped parcel in Bridgehampton on the east end of Long Island in 1987. Formerly a potato field, the land offered him a chance to build a new home and a garden.

While planning the Colonial-style house with an architect from Richmond, Virginia, John also began to lay out the 2-acre landscape. He knew that in order for the home to look established, it needed to be surrounded by mature gardens. "I measured everything and staked off the 'rooms,'" he explains. "I worked it so you can walk along one side of the garden and feel as if you're walking such a distance that you don't realize there's more until you enter the next area."

John planted mixed hedges of flowering shrubs and deciduous and evergreen trees around the perimeter, creating a verdant backdrop to the interior garden and also serving as a windbreak to protect plants when storms roll in from the Atlantic. There's a pleasing formality to the garden, with its crab apple *allée*, borders framed by espaliered apple trees, paths laid with ancient round millstones, and portals flanked by obelisks. No fewer than eighteen magnolia trees with yellow,

"There are moments in my garden when I am overwhelmed by happiness."

ABOVE: With cottage-style double-hung windows painted white, the bump-out nook reminds John that the inspiration for his potting shed was originally a fisherman's miniscule home. He's added two marble spheres at the foundation's edge and perched a carved figure in front of the shingled siding.

RIGHT: When viewed across the brilliant green swath of lawn, the shed's lines and angles are visually appealing. The hinged barn doors, at right, open for rolling a wheelbarrow inside or out. Appearing as if they were randomly tossed here, oversized fruit sculptures almost dwarf the scene. BELOW: The cupola was copied detail-for-detail from an eighteenth-century hut that caught John's eye. He added an antique weather vane from his collection.

OWNER
John Barham

DESIGN
ARCHITECTURE: John Barham

CONSTRUCTION: Arthur Peterson

LANDSCAPE: John Barham

white, and pink blooms reside in this garden, along with columnar red beeches, dawn redwoods, red chestnuts, blue spruces, and golden sequoias.

Filling the landscape with beloved trees and shrubs was only the beginning for John. Indeed, he has populated the grounds with hundreds of stone, marble, and bronze sculptures commissioned over the years from Asia. There are carved Buddhas and Korean soldiers; a crane, seahorse, and carp cast in bronze; stone faces and dancing frogs. "Luckily, there isn't space for any more," John quips, while showing visitors a photograph of a monkey sculpture he's just commissioned.

John needed a place to store tools and equipment, but of course it had to be architecturally interesting (even the small pool house is designed to resemble an eighteenth-century Virginia cookhouse, complete with chimney). On frequent trips to Long Island's North Fork, John admired a fisherman's shingled tiny house. "I loved its design, including the angle of the roof and its little porch," he recalls. "To me, it had such style."

A builder reproduced the hut from John's sketches, finishing its exterior with the same southern cypress shingles used on the main house. Measuring about 15 by 20 feet, with a bump-out room next to the front door, the shed brings delight to anyone who sees it. Its storybook appearance allowed John to decorate the exterior surfaces with his collections, from whimsical birdhouses to vintage farming implements to maritime objects. A cupola with tiny nooks for birds is topped with an antique weather vane, one of an extensive collection mounted above John's garage.

Inside, there are shelves and counters for John's essentials, including pruning sheers and loppers, trowels, cultivators, hoes, rakes, and shovels. His vintage watering cans are gathered here, collected over the years and kept long after they've begun to rust. Glass cloches of every size are on hand for protecting tender spring bulbs from rabbits or birds. A stash of flowerpots and bags of potting soil are ready for year-round planting projects. "It drives me crazy when I read about all these new plants," says John, who maintains a brisk correspondence with favorite nurseries on both coasts. "I no longer have room to grow anything new."

John rarely leaves his home and garden for overnight trips, preferring to connect with the larger world through his ever-expanding collection of sculpture, not to mention borders filled with plants native to both hemispheres. "The garden is for me, a great romance," John says. "Think of any great romance in your life—the joy, love, creation, nurturing, frustration, and intimacy— and you will understand, and know, my garden."

ABOVE LEFT: Pruners in hand in case he needs to clip a wayward stem, John Barham takes daily strolls through his pristine 2-acre landscape. He has devoted two decades to this property, personally selecting every tree and shrub specimen and adding an ever-expanding menagerie of sculpture. CENTER AND RIGHT: A brass "beast" doubles as a doorknocker; a weathered birdhouse, painted to read BARHAM'S MARKET, was given to John as a gift.

MATERIALS
ROOF: cypress shingles

EXTERIOR: hand-cut cypress shingles; white tongue-and-groove boards on porch

INTERIOR WALLS: smooth drywall painted white

WINDOWS: double-hung, wood-framed, painted white

DOOR: white plank with wrought-iron hardware

FLOOR: poured cement

HILL COUNTRY HAVEN

BUILT FROM LIMESTONE ROCK CHARACTERISTIC OF OLD TEXAS FARMHOUSES, A POTTING SHED OCCUPIES THE HEART AND SOUL OF A COUNTRY GARDEN

Previously urban dwellers, Sylvia and Steven Williams created a weekend place in Bertram, Texas: population 1,100. It didn't take long for "Stonebridge," with its potting shed, extensive gardens, and pair of longhorn steers, to become their full-time occupation.

ABOVE: During spring, Texas Hill Country's roadsides and meadows are carpeted by carefree native wildflowers in a rainbow of hues, including this vibrant gold-and-crimson blanket flower *Gaillardia sp.* OPPOSITE: A jaunty rooster weather vane, originally Sylvia's father's, is perched on a cupola that tops the red metal roof. Made of limestone rock, Sylvia and Steven's 400-square-foot structure is used for everything from messy gardening projects to serving a champagne brunch. Their daily routine includes dawn and dusk visits to their garden getaway.

It's a long way, physically and psychologically, from an Austin town house to Burnet County, Texas. "Let's just say I'm here thanks to Sylvia's latent desire to have a garden," deadpans Steven Williams, an executive recruiter. "We have the proverbial five-day-a-week hobby that everyone wishes they had."

For Steven, that "dream" frequently involves hauling bags of mulch and cattle feed, or riding his Gator tractor to deliver hay to the barn. The Williamses' semiretired rural existence suits them. Married in 1998, they left their metropolitan lifestyle and moved to a country address on a farm-to-market road, one of hundreds throughout Texas's agricultural communities.

MISSION
To construct a personal building that's "practical and pretty" for housing garden tools, displaying botanical collections, and entertaining friends

MUST-HAVES
A potting area and a sink, old windows and doors, a front porch and an arbor, a workbench

INSPIRATION
Stone farmhouses and outbuildings of Texas Hill Country, circa 1850

DESIGN CHALLENGES
To create an attractive garden building that satisfies his-and-her activities: a "retreat" for her, a workshop for him

CREATIVE SOLUTIONS
She wanted to clad the 400-square-foot shed with salvaged barn wood; he thought it should be finished in limestone rock like their house. As a compromise, they used stone for the exterior and lined interior walls with wide planks from an aging barn. Furnishings share functional and festive purposes: the desk can accommodate lunch for four; the workbench becomes a cocktail bar; the potting bench is used for buffet service.

For three years, Sylvia searched for property within a 50-mile radius of Austin. "I wanted acreage for privacy," she explains. They bought the two-story limestone farmhouse several years after Sylvia first viewed it. "It was only going to be our weekend place, but we moved here permanently in 1999," she says.

After years running several businesses in Austin, including a commercial bank, a travel agency, and Flowers to Go, a floral business, Sylvia is content to spend her time gardening. Her love for horticulture and flower arranging led Sylvia to study as a Master Gardener; she is president of Highland Lakes Master Gardeners, a local group in Burnet County.

In order to create Stonebridge Gardens, the one-acre series of borders, islands, and flower beds, Sylvia first needed to clear away a tangle of mesquite trees and plow the soil. She allowed two mesquites to remain, with plans to incorporate them into the future garden. At the center of the cleared land, she designated space for the potting shed; the 18-by-22 structure is set

on a slight angle to face the driveway. Long ago envisioned in her imagination, Sylvia wanted the potting shed to look like it had been here forever.

Construction almost came to a standstill, though, while Sylvia and Steven "negotiated" key design choices. "I thought we could use barn wood on the exterior and Steven said, 'No, I want us to finish it in limestone because it goes with our house,'" Sylvia recalls. "He convinced me that we should use the rock, but I was determined to cover it with vines!"

Along with eight hinged windows, two doors, a ceiling fan, a concrete floor, and a vine-covered entry, the stone contributes to cooler inside temperatures during hot Texas summer months. Even in the dead of winter, there are days when the sun pouring through the windows makes time in the shed enjoyable.

Stonebridge is a frequent stop for local tours and garden club visits. Each spring, Sylvia hosts the graduating class of new

ABOVE LEFT: Salvaged windows appear on all four sides of the shed; with a top hinge, they can be propped open with a stick to allow cross breezes to cool the interior. When Sylvia conceded to Steven's choice of a limestone rock exterior, she lined the inside walls with planks rescued from an aging Texas barn. RIGHT: A vintage window, suspended from a garden arbor, creates the illusion of an inviting outdoor room.

"I always wanted to find a place in the country—a retreat. And for years, I had plans for this potting shed in my mind."

—SYLVIA WILLIAMS

OWNERS
Steven and Sylvia Williams

DESIGN
ARCHITECTURE: Sylvia McCasland
Williams

BUILDER/CONTRACTOR: Brad
McCasland and Paul Solis

LANDSCAPE: Sylvia McCasland
Williams

CLOCKWISE FROM LEFT: In Sylvia's garden, an herb-and-vegetable bed with a sun dial at its center is edged in pieces of limestone rock similar to her garden shed exterior; swathed in a perennial clematis vine, one of several arbors provides entry to Stonebridge Gardens, the oft-toured garden that Sylvia and Steven began creating in 1999; the dew of dawn appears on a perfectly shaped artichoke.

Master Gardener trainees. She and Steven share their garden as a way to educate fellow enthusiasts about organic practices, gardening for birds and wildlife, native Texas plants, and growing ornamental and edible plants together.

Their labor of love even makes an impression on non-gardeners. Often, when the couple entertains, the shed serves as the setting for evening cocktails or after-dinner drinks. A floral tablecloth transforms the workbench into a bar. The doors and windows remain propped open to the garden's nighttime sounds—crickets sing to the backdrop of a bubbling pond and the long-horns call to each other in the pasture.

Women and men alike are drawn to this setting, which is equal parts rugged and romantic. "It's wonderful to hear the comments whenever someone new walks inside," Sylvia says. "We love sharing it."

LEFT, FROM TOP: According to this road sign, Bertram, Texas, has a population of 1,122, including Steven and Sylvia Williams, former city folk who have embraced their country lifestyle; a barbed-wire circle is a poignant addition to a wooden cross that Sylvia has hung in the shed; the rooster weather vane stands proud against the intense blue Texas sky.

BELOW: Sylvia sits at this desk while planning seasonal projects, checking reference books, and ordering seeds, but it can also accommodate four for lunch.

MATERIALS
ROOF: red standing-seam metal with antique weather vane

EXTERIOR: limestone rock

INTERIOR WALLS: salvaged barn wood

WINDOWS/DOOR: architectural salvage

FLOOR: stained concrete

A ROOM WITH A VIEW

CONSTRUCTED WITH A HODGEPODGE OF FORTY-THREE GLASS WINDOWS AND DOORS, JENNIE HAMMILL'S SPARKLING GARDEN HOUSE IS THE PERFECT PLACE TO TAKE TEA AND OBSERVE HER PLANTS AND RESIDENT BIRDLIFE

A concert pianist is drawn to fine woodworking as a tangible expression of her creativity.

ABOVE: A carved bird by Seattle artist Michael Zitka perches on a ledge inside Jennie and Tully Hammill's glass "teahouse." OPPOSITE: When illuminated at dawn, the distinct shape of each window and door that forms the 10-by-14-foot building is outlined in sharp detail. Jennie salvaged and recycled many of the frames and built 20-inch-square windows with crossed mullions to wrap around the clerestory below the roof.

Jennie Hammill supports herself by combining two professions that others may find incongruous: she teaches piano students ages six to seventy-six at side-by-side grand pianos in her living room, and runs Ballard Woodworks, a custom cabinet–building business in her 1,100-square-foot basement shop. Music and woodworking require equal parts discipline and free expression, explains the petite blonde. "It's the combination of aural and visual," she concedes. "I need a balance of both."

MISSION
To create a miniature glass conservatory for privacy and seclusion in a city garden

MUST-HAVES
Walls made from salvaged windows in a variety of styles and sizes; a bench that converts into a day-bed; places for reading, serving tea, and enjoying meals; niches for display-ing collections; a conserva-tory roof; interior lighting; and a weatherproof floor

INSPIRATION
A whimsical garden house—made from recycled windows, stained glass, and shutters—designed by Jennie's neighbor Randy Keller, a landscape archi-tect. She enlisted him to help her create something similar for her own backyard.

DESIGN CHALLENGES
To design and build a 124-square-foot building entirely out of glass; to situate it in such a way

that it didn't overpower a 40-by-108-foot city lot but maximized garden views

CREATIVE SOLUTIONS
Jennie placed her "teahouse" near the south property line of her back-yard, at the foot of three large Douglas fir trees. The structure is aligned to capture two major sight lines: looking west along the side garden and east toward the patio garden.

OPPOSITE: A pair of red French doors frames the entrance, drawing guests inside where a cushion-covered bench and other comfortable seating furnish the interiors. There is a pleasing contrast between the rugged concrete-paved floor and the attractive ceiling fixture more likely to appear in a formal dining room. Jennie wanted the structure's proportions to accommodate six for dinner or a buffet service that might spill out into the garden.

ABOVE LEFT: Brunch is set at a drop-leaf table that Jennie refinished to match the room's butter-colored interior. She and Tully enjoy dining here where they can observe favorite plants, visiting birds, and the passage of the seasons. RIGHT: Jennie appropriated vintage windows and another set of French doors to design and build a playful shed for storing tools and flowerpots. She says its 3-by-5-foot dimensions remind her of a telephone booth in England; the peaked copper roof is topped with a ball finial and painted with a cheerful scheme that complements the teahouse.

OPPOSITE, LEFT: A bird motif appears on top of a round accent table placed in front of the window. RIGHT: Jennie's artistic talents extend to making glass and tile mosaics, with which she often adorns furniture of her own design. She found a piece of checkerboard tile sheeting and fashioned a mosaic window box for herbs.

Called "Miss Jennie" by piano students young and old, she picked up saws, planes, and chisels long after she became familiar with a piano keyboard. While earning her doctorate in piano performance at the University of Washington, Jennie visited a woodworking class at a Seattle community college. "It was the coolest thing," she recalls. "I felt like a kid in a candy shop. I remember thinking, This is what I want."

Smelling fresh-cut wood and feeling sawdust beneath her shoes triggered for Jennie favorite memories of helping her father in his woodshop. She was in her late thirties when this life-changing new chapter opened up. "During my first quarter at woodworking school, I also defended my dissertation," Jennie recalls.

There is plenty of evidence of Jennie's gift for fine cabinetmaking in the two-story 1926 Seattle cottage she shares with her husband, Tully, a retired computer programmer. The kitchen cupboards, the bathroom vanity, bookcases, and tables

are among the many home improvement projects she's undertaken.

Walk outside and enter her small city garden where an extraordinary example of her carpentry stands. Working around her piano-teaching schedule, this gifted musician-turned-woodworker constructed a miniature glass conservatory. Both delicate and substantial, Jennie's "teahouse" is where she enjoys quiet moments sharing cups of English Breakfast or Earl Grey tea with friends, reading, and finding respite without leaving home.

An avid gardener who is active in the Northwest Perennial Alliance, Jennie found it difficult to keep plants alive beneath the three Douglas firs that tower above the south side of her garden. "My motto is that if you can't get anything to grow in a spot, build something there," she says with a knowing grin. And soon she found the solution to a fallow patch of earth: a tiny garden conservatory built by her neighbor Randolph Scott

"I'm impressed by the amazing qualities of glass. From the outside, you can look into the building, beyond it to the plants on the other side, and still see a reflection of the garden behind you— all at the same time. The glass plays with the light and obscures reality."

Keller, a landscape architect. Measuring about 7 by 8 feet, with a small vestibule at either end, Keller's tiny garden house not only appealed to Jennie but also got her thinking about how to construct one of her own.

Keller created the structure using a large stained-glass window from an ancient church in Spain and other salvaged windows. He and his wife, Victoria, enjoy views of their summer garden from here and add holiday decorations to the little building come December. "It's like a jewel to reflect light back into the garden," he says.

Jennie's teahouse enhances what was once an uninspiring section of the garden. From its location beneath the fir trees, she enjoys "the longest views our property has to offer." With Keller as her designer and "coach," Jennie spent most of the summer of 2004 building the glass house; she finished it the following spring.

She excavated soil to place the finished structure "low and settled in the garden, amid the plants." This feeling is reinforced by deep borders of ornamental trees, shrubs, and perennials that grow along the east and west sides. Jennie has trained climbing vines to scramble up to the roof's edge and twist around a horizontal strip of wood added for that purpose.

Jennie amassed vintage windows to form the walls of the main 10-by-10-foot structure and a 6-by-4-foot bump-out on one side. She also found windows with leaded glass, divided panes, and even a cottage-style one made from thirty tiny squares of glass; most of them cost only $5 to $20. She cut old glass frames to fit necessary sizes and custom-built a dozen 20-inch-square windows, each with two crossed mullions. These charming pieces surround the sides of a second-tier clerestory so that even more light floods the interior space. The design echoes windows seen on Seattle's famed Volunteer Park Conservatory, a Victorian-era glass house erected in 1912.

OWNERS
Jennie and Tully Hammill

DESIGN
ARCHITECTURE:
Randolph Scott Keller, ASLA Landscape Architecture

CONSTRUCTION/ CARPENTRY: Jennie Hammill, Ballard Woodworks

LANDSCAPE:
Jennie Hammill

Jennie attached the window-walls to 12-foot-tall corner posts set in concrete footings. "I used clamps and little boards to hold things in place while I bolted them together," she explains. She finished the lower portion of interior walls with wainscoting and covered the floor with reddish pavers set in sand. The blue gray exterior paint is a good color to complement Jennie's golden full-moon Japanese maple tree planted in the garden.

Jennie and Tully love to dine here together or with friends. They pull a round table to the center of the teahouse so two people can sit on a built-in bench made by Jennie and four others can use chairs. A buffet is laid out on the potting bench inside an adjacent toolshed, a fanciful structure that Jennie also created. "We come here in the late afternoon or evening. The sun arrives from the west and it feels toasty warm inside because the stone floor holds the heat."

While she first worried that the teahouse would crowd her garden, Jennie says it has done the opposite. "I thought it would make the garden look totally minuscule, but the garden feels more spacious now," she says.

MATERIALS
ROOF: rolled composite

WALLS: recycled/ salvaged windows; interiors finished with wainscoting

CLERESTORY WINDOWS: 20-inch square with two crossed mullions, custom-made by Jennie Hammill

DOOR: 10-pane wood-framed French doors painted red

FLOOR: sand-set tumbled concrete pavers

LEFT: Comfortable pillows on the built-in bench ensure that moments inside the teahouse are enjoyable whether Jennie is reading or taking afternoon tea. She designed the hinged bench to fold open into a full-size platform bed meant for dozing.

OPPOSITE: Another carved bird by Michael Zitka has wire legs and boldly holds a berry in its beak. Jennie added millwork to the interior shelf to echo the crossed-mullion window design.

HEART OF THE COUNTRY

A NORTHWEST COUPLE COLLECTS FRAGMENTS OF THE PAST, EXHIBITING THEM IN A CAREFREE GARDEN

Collectors of late-nineteenth- and early-twentieth-century antiques,

Janie and Billy Fowler use a cluster of vintage sheds to bring

a slice of Americana to their garden.

ABOVE: A hand-lettered sign on a piece of broken siding hangs from a rusty wire. OPPOSITE: With an amiable gable, the 10-by-10-foot storage shed is a weathered canvas on which Janie and Billy Fowler hang many of their vintage tools and farm implements. Janie uses the shed's shady side to display a collection of painted sap buckets planted with yellow-blooming begonias. At the foot of this scene grow lush green hostas. FOLLOWING PAGE: An aging washtub is planted with herbs and annuals; crushed hazelnut shells carpet the ground.

Janie and Billy Fowler have designed their garden in phases, corner by corner, inspired by ideas from country towns they have visited throughout America. Instead of vacations, the couple goes on "junking" expeditions to garage sales and auctions in search of antiques to display on their one-acre property in Maltby, a rural community about 30 miles north of Seattle.

Whenever Janie dreams up a backyard structure, her husband and son, both in the construction trade, find the time and materials to turn it into something tangible. Four miniature buildings—three sheds and a mill house—dot the landscape. Rustic-looking but well-constructed, they reside near a stream or among a stand of foxgloves and a mound of herbs. "I like primitive, and that's what Billy and Johnny can do," Janie explains.

MISSION
To populate a storybook landscape with four small-scale cabins for storing tools and displaying antique objects

MUST-HAVES
Interiors dedicated to storing patio furniture, garden tools, and flowerpots, with authentic exteriors—salvaged barn wood, vintage windows and doors, and cedar shake roofing

INSPIRATION
An appreciation for the pioneer homes of the past—and a love for primitive objects

DESIGN CHALLENGE
To give each shed a timeless appearance so that it looks as if it had been there for a century

CREATIVE SOLUTIONS
Janie and Billy spent weekends scouring back roads and junkyards in search of "building material" salvaged from decrepit barns and fences. They discovered castoffs from what others considered useless, and in turn gave each found object a special place in their backyard.

"I like to use the not-so-obvious things, so none of my friends throw anything away until they ask me first."

—JANIE FOWLER

ABOVE LEFT: On a French bistro table rests a 1940s jug containing just-cut lilies and sprays of chartreuse lady's mantle; an array of zinc pitch pots is scattered on the shelf above. RIGHT: With chipped paint recalling earlier days, a windmill adorns a corner of the flower-and-herb garden.

The outbuildings are the perfect vehicle for displaying collections: vintage tools, farm implements, salvaged barnyard finds, and antique café furniture. Each item tells a story. When asked its provenance, Janie draws her visitors to a nesting box or a sap bucket or even a feeding trough, spinning a tale about the hands that must have once used it.

Two events prompted the Fowlers' sudden interest in their landscape. First, an extensive home addition, to add a commercial kitchen and an office wing for Janie's catering business, required ripping up and renovating the side yard. Second, with their son grown, the couple decided it was time to convert an outdoor tennis court into a usable garden, with raised planting beds and a play area for grandchildren.

To avoid the expense of demolishing the tennis court, they worked instead with its parameters. Janie encouraged English ivy to engulf the chain-link fence, creating in the process a lush wall of green to surround the south side of the garden.

Ten raised beds, constructed without "bottoms" and resting on the tennis court's original surface, provide areas to grow flowers and vegetables. Pathways between the beds are formed by deep layers of crushed hazelnut shells, a favorite local resource. "I love the soothing sound of walking here," Janie says. "You can hear that crackle underneath your feet."

With a charming gabled roof and dormer, a humbly named "storage shed" occupies one corner of the tennis court. Janie asked her son, Johnny Fowler, owner of International General Contractors, to build the 10-by-10-foot building. An architectural focal point for the surrounding cutting garden, it provides an out-of-the-way place to store patio furniture. Old rakes and long-handled tools are displayed across the front—readily available for tending to plants.

In need of a spot for more garden tools and bags of compost, Janie envisioned a potting shed near her kitchen garden. The 8-by-8-foot scaled-down barn incorporates a pair of beveled

ABOVE LEFT: A dusty lantern hangs from a hook in front of the carriage house window. The Fowlers use the structure to store their antique sleigh. RIGHT: Precise lettering gives a piece of picket fencing new life as a whimsical sign.

OWNERS
Janie and Billy Fowler

DESIGN ARCHITECTURE:
Janie Fowler

CONSTRUCTION: Johnny
Fowler, International
General Contractors

LANDSCAPE: Janie and
Billy Fowler

**WATER WHEEL/DRY
CREEK:** Nick Sands,
Nature's Way Land-
scape and Design

TOP: The potting shed roof is partially
obscured by akebia and clematis vines
while morning light dances across a
row of foxgloves, prized by Janie for
their ability to self-sow in unexpected
places.

ABOVE: A ledge holds tarnished but
cherished spray nozzles that Janie and
Billy have picked up over the years.

and leaded glass windows salvaged from one of Billy's renovation sites. Mounted on an exterior wall is a series of hen-
nesting boxes, now used for storing different-size terra-cotta
pots. The interior is furnished with a basin-style sink and
shelves for tools and fertilizer. "The front door came from an
old chicken coop, and the big window was salvaged from a
school that was being torn down," Janie explains.

Recycled barn wood and cedar shakes give the shed its
authenticity. With a deep-pitched porch roof covered in clematis and akebia vines, the structure provides a shady place to sit
while savoring mouthfuls of just-picked strawberries. Perhaps
it really is a hundred-year-old shack once occupied by an early
settler who arrived on the Oregon Trail.

Janie grows herbs, berries, and vegetables to supply her
catering endeavors. Borage, basil, rosemary, lavender, and
other culinary and aromatic plants fill the raised beds. Rhu-
barb, peas, beans, and lettuces grow in tidy rows. She harvests
flowers throughout the garden to garnish dishes and create floral arrangements for clients' tables.

Billy constructed a third shed to house an antique sleigh
that he and Janie purchased from a local antiques dealer. To
situate it, he walked around the property with a bamboo stake,

> "I don't like shiny, chrome, or highly polished surfaces. Give me something old and I'll find a use for it."
>
> —JANIE FOWLER

marking the ideal place that Janie could see from her kitchen window. The 10-by-12-foot building's roof extends to shelter the sleigh, which was once pulled by horses.

"The plans for these sheds began on napkins," Janie confides. Part decorative, part utilitarian, the wee buildings lend history to the twenty-first-century garden. They serve as a fitting backdrop for rustic collections: old barrels, wagon wheels, turned posts with chipped paint, rusted watering cans. To speed up the aging of cedar siding, Janie mixes a cup of baking soda into a gallon of water. "I wash the wood with this mixture, and within days, it turns gray," she says. "It gives my sheds a jump start on weathering, although there is nothing better than letting Mother Nature do her trick."

Adorning the front yard is a tiny "mill house," an 8-by-8-foot building built from cedar and stone. A hand-painted sign reads: FOWLER CREEK HOLLOW. The tin roof was reconstructed from an old barn in nearby Snohomish County, and a rotating wheel pours water into a man-made creek. "I remember seeing waterwheels on grist mills in the country," Janie says. "It is a comforting feeling to see it go 'round."

Likewise, when visitors arrive here, they put the modern world behind them. "People tell us it's like walking back one hundred years in time to a little village," Janie says. "I think we all need to be reminded of our humble beginnings—these sheds are part of our history."

Morning and evening, the Fowlers find themselves drawn to the brick patio outside their living room. They hear leaves from the Virginia creeper rustle in the breeze, drink in the fragrance of the garden, and listen to the soft music of water that flows over a bed of Fraser River rock.

"We have a glass of wine in our hands and we go from one café table to another bench," Janie says. "I ask Billy, 'Why would we want to leave and go on vacation?'"

ABOVE: Janie used chalk to spell out SEEDS & FLOWERS on a broken piece of slate. It hangs, appropriately, by the potting shed door.

MATERIALS
ROOF: cedar shake and salvaged tin

EXTERIOR: salvaged barn wood

WINDOWS/DOOR: architectural salvage

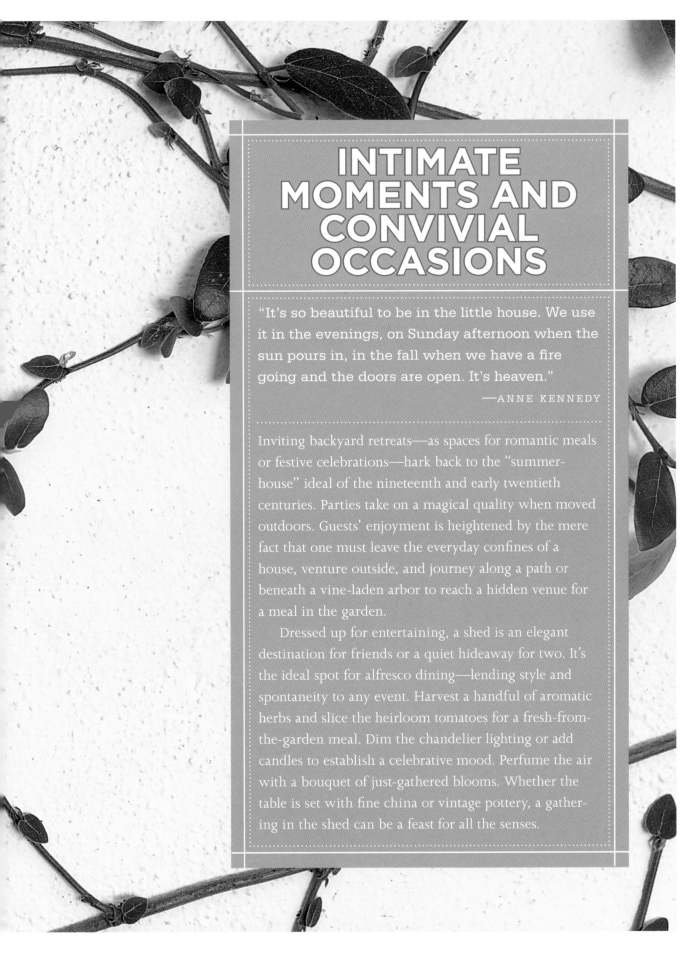

INTIMATE MOMENTS AND CONVIVIAL OCCASIONS

"It's so beautiful to be in the little house. We use it in the evenings, on Sunday afternoon when the sun pours in, in the fall when we have a fire going and the doors are open. It's heaven."

—ANNE KENNEDY

Inviting backyard retreats—as spaces for romantic meals or festive celebrations—hark back to the "summerhouse" ideal of the nineteenth and early twentieth centuries. Parties take on a magical quality when moved outdoors. Guests' enjoyment is heightened by the mere fact that one must leave the everyday confines of a house, venture outside, and journey along a path or beneath a vine-laden arbor to reach a hidden venue for a meal in the garden.

Dressed up for entertaining, a shed is an elegant destination for friends or a quiet hideaway for two. It's the ideal spot for alfresco dining—lending style and spontaneity to any event. Harvest a handful of aromatic herbs and slice the heirloom tomatoes for a fresh-from-the-garden meal. Dim the chandelier lighting or add candles to establish a celebrative mood. Perfume the air with a bouquet of just-gathered blooms. Whether the table is set with fine china or vintage pottery, a gathering in the shed can be a feast for all the senses.

SWEET RETREAT

A GEM OF A GARDEN ROOM IS QUIET AND COMFORTABLE, YET SEPARATE FROM THE MAIN HOUSE

Two designers create an interior sanctuary furnished
with antiques, Chinese silk pillows,
luxurious linens, and a vintage 1920s chandelier.

ABOVE: An embroidered dragonfly adorns the linen slipcovers.
OPPOSITE: Like peering into an old-world diorama, Tony Nahra and Rand Babcock's garden room is a magical space that transforms its occupants. "I feel like it's our little retreat in a different world," Rand confides. Like a piece of sculpture, the marble pedestal table is the room's artful focal point. Framed in recycled barn wood, the oversize mirror plays the role of a picture window, reflecting the verdant garden palette into the space.

ABOVE: Filled with collections from their travels to Asia and Europe, the garden house is like Rand and Tony's personal treasure box. They designed the 10-by-10-foot space as an urban backyard getaway but find it's an appealing place for entertaining friends. A pair of 15-pane French doors, painted in celadon green to contrast with the home's black trim, opens onto an outdoor patio where a teak dining set accommodates larger gatherings. When Tony and Rand wish for quieter meals, they invite two or three friends to join them inside.

"The moment I enter, I'm in a different world."

—RAND BABCOCK

Rand's grandmother created an elaborate wooden box for each of her grandchildren. Finished on the inside with decoupage and on the outside with gilded papier-mâché, the ornate containers stored cherished photographs and family mementos. "She saved things from our childhood in those boxes and kept little stories in them," he recalls.

In a similar way, Rand Babock and Tony Nahra's garden room is a treasure-filled hideaway they enjoy alone or with friends. Rand describes it as "a place to collect memories, experiences—and some of our favorite objects."

MISSION
To create a secret destination in an urban backyard

MUST-HAVES
Daybed, dining table, chandelier

INSPIRATION
A handmade "memory box" filled with keepsakes and family heirlooms

DESIGN CHALLENGE
To make the most of a dark 100-square-foot space. "We wanted our ten-by-ten-foot room to fulfill multiple purposes, including serving dinner for six or taking a nap," Rand says.

CREATIVE SOLUTIONS
Two skylights, one recycled cottage window, and a pair of 8-foot French doors invite light inside. An oversize mirror reflects the garden's greenery and serves as a faux window on a dark interior wall.

OWNERS
Rand Babcock and Tony Nahra

DESIGN
INTERIOR: Rand Babcock, Legacy
Creations

LANDSCAPE: Daniel Lowery, Queen
Anne Gardens

friends over, they usually ask if we can dine in the garden room." The journey begins when the hosts and their guests walk through the kitchen door and descend to the garden via an outdoor staircase. Carrying armloads of wineglasses and plates, trays of cheeses, fruits, and breads, and a bowl of pasta, they stroll through two paved terraces—one a circle and the other a square—before arriving at their destination.

Despite its small footprint, the space has a feeling of largesse, thanks to the pillow-laden iron daybed, the slip-covered chairs, and the oversize mirror (another flea market discovery). At first, the men used a collapsible café table for meals, but "we realized that everybody wants to eat in this room and we needed something solid," Rand says. "The table's size was okay, but when you put four people with wineglasses around it we worried about even one bump."

Tony and Rand opted for an elegant 36-inch Italian pedestal table made from honed antique breccia marble, found through an Internet source. "The marble pulls in all the colors, from the cool gray plaster walls to the warm pillow silks," Rand explains. "Plus, it weighs four hundred pounds, and it will be here when the house falls down."

Dressed with candles and stemware, the table is just the right size for a small dinner party. Rand and Tony invite guests to perch on the bed cushions or café chairs and join them for a menu that includes fresh berries and dishes seasoned with herbs Tony harvests from the garden. Light from the lanterns is reflected in the mirror and chandelier crystals, adding sparkle to the room.

The laughter of friends harmonizes with the subtle music of water trickling in a nearby garden fountain. "It's intimate," Tony confides. "It's a space that transforms your mood when you enter."

MATERIALS

EXTERIOR: cedar shake siding to match house

ROOF: composite shingles

SKYLIGHTS: polycarbonate

CEILING: tongue-and-groove decking and exposed beams; custom color stain

INTERIOR WALLS: custom hand-rubbed plaster finish

SIDE WINDOW: original to home and salvaged from kitchen renovation

DOORS: 8-foot, 18-pane cedar French doors

FLOORS: 6-inch sand-set Roman block pavers

RIGHT: The room's small proportions heighten the enjoyment of anyone who enters. Tony and Rand enjoy sharing the space with their friends, including Jeanine Burke and Michi Suzuki, another couple in their dinner group. On a warm summer night, as the sun sets, the scene is set for frivolity or quiet conversation—or both.

OPPOSITE, LEFT: Adjacent to the garden room and paved with the same stone, the square terrace defines a distinct space for alfresco occasions. TOP: Rand and Tony designed their garden room as a private retreat, reached through a pair of French doors.

EXTRAVAGANT GESTURES

STANDING TALL IN A CACTUS- AND SUCCULENT-FILLED LANDSCAPE, A GOLDEN PAVILION COMMANDS ATTENTION AND OFFERS DAZZLING VIEWS OF THE VISTA BEYOND

Like an outdoor theater designed with a dramatic collection

of aloes and agaves, the gold-stucco-and-red-tile pavilion sets the stage

for Patrick Anderson and Les Olson's garden gatherings.

ABOVE: In keeping with Patrick's sun-drenched design palette, an aloe reveals its electric-orange blooms. OPPOSITE: Poised at the highest place on the 2-acre property and partially hidden by tall pine trees, barbed cactuses, and colorful succulents, the grand pavilion is a must-visit destination for its owners and their visitors. *Revelation,* a rusted steel figure by artist Joseph Kinnebrew, lends texture and form to the setting. When Patrick and Les entertain, they and guests fill picnic baskets with refreshments, stroll through the garden, and arrive at the pavilion for evening cocktails.

After they retired from careers in law and human resources, respectively, Les Olson and Patrick Anderson left Pasadena for "the country"—a 2-acre parcel in Fallbrook, California, in northern San Diego County. Patrick seized the chance to invent his own plant world here, spending the past fifteen years shaping the landscape with unusual spiked, whorled, spherical, and fan-shaped cactuses, along with succulents representing a color spectrum from maroon to bronze to silvery blue. "Every inch of this property is plantable if I ever get around to it," he maintains. The garden's finishing touch: a golden open-air pavilion where Les and Patrick seek haven from heat and sun.

MISSION
To give a desert landscape an architectural point of view where its owners can enjoy shelter from sun and heat

MUST-HAVES
Building elements that echo those of the primary house, including square stucco columns and terracotta roof tiles; space for a dining table to seat six to eight guests; a grand staircase for extra seating and displaying potted plants; a whimsical rooftop finial

INSPIRATION
Patrick sketched the pavilion as a dramatic nonplant element for his oft-photographed landscape. "It needed to make sense with what was here, though: a sweet Victorian gazebo wasn't going to cut it," he explains.

DESIGN CHALLENGES
To create a striking structure that fits comfortably into the landscape

CREATIVE SOLUTIONS
The staircase, which accommodates a steep grade change and gradually ascends from the garden to the dining area, has 16-inch-deep treads and 6-inch risers

The neighbors jokingly call it the Taj Mahal, but the opulant pavilion situated at the highest point of Patrick and Les's property has exactly the right degree of dramatic presence their flamboyant desert garden needs. Together the structure and plant collections embody Patrick's two loves: theater and horticulture.

A third-generation California native, Patrick learned to garden at the knee of his Irish grandmother Mary Agnes Anderson. "She had the most beautiful roses you'd ever seen," he recalls. "I caught the gardening bug from her and went on from there." By the time Patrick was twelve, an eccentric neighbor introduced him to desert plants. "He was one of those collectors who had ten million pots of cactus along the edges of his driveway," recalls Patrick, who began to grow his own collection of epiphyllum (orchid cactus) in pots.

While attending the University of Redlands, Patrick studied theater, directing, and costume design. "After college, I forsook

BELOW: Patrick wanted to situate the pavilion so that it could be seen from house and garden alike. He designed it with two open sides, capturing views of his exotic plantings and distant hills. The remaining sides face neighboring properties, so they are walled to create privacy, although small arched windows provide a glimpse of sculpture and plants beyond. In keeping with the structure's massive scale, a well-proportioned ceiling lantern and two sconces establish an intimate mood at dusk. The wide staircase serves as impromptu seating for large gatherings.

ABOVE LEFT: The round silhouette of a 40-inch concrete urn is a pleasing counterpoint to the spiked agave and euphorbia growing at its base. Patrick placed a series of three Lunaform urns, chosen for their terra-cotta coloring and "massive scale," amid plantings of cactus and succulents. RIGHT: Over paprika-colored linen, the table is set to serve brunch for four. When he and Les entertain, Patrick creates tabletop schemes with festive 1940s Bauer pottery. Highly collectible, the American-made bowls, platters, vases, and plates are finished in playful shades of turquoise, burnt orange, jade, and Chinese yellow. A vintage McCoy "Oil Jar" from the same era is a stunning container for a spray of flowers that echo the pottery glazes.

theater for something that actually paid the bills and ended up working in human resources at a big accounting firm in Los Angeles," he says. "But I've continued to sing opera and early music." He also volunteered each week at the famed Huntington Botanical Gardens, where he rediscovered the desert plants he grew as a child and learned to propagate them.

Les, Patrick's partner, is a former state superior court judge who was born in Chicago but came to California to attend Stanford Law School and never left. In 1988, anticipating Les's retirement, the men looked for a place to live outside the city and eventually narrowed their search to Fallbrook, a town about six miles inland from the Pacific Ocean. "We knew we wanted a place where we could actually have a garden," Patrick says. The original landscaping was not a tabula rasa, however. Surrounding a 1970s California-style ranch house was a mixed citrus grove, ubiquitous ice plant, and what Patrick refers to as "gas station plants"—clumps of agapanthus and fortnight lilies. Forty lime trees populated the upper garden, about thirty-eight more than Patrick and Les needed in any given year. After

removing most of the citrus trees and prosaic plantings, the men installed no fewer than 250 ornamental trees, many of them seedlings or young trees in one-gallon nursery pots. Now, nearly twenty years later, a eucalyptus grove, Italian stone and Torrey pines, Kashmir cypress, Catalina ironwood, and an African fever tree tower above the rooftops, providing shade and skyline interest.

Patrick designed paths to meander through the garden and lead to a dramatic destination. "I wanted the walk to circle through the garden—and these two main paths made them-selves obvious to me, winding around the edges and meeting at the pavilion," he explains. "As a strolling garden, it encour-ages people to slow down and enjoy the route from plant to plant." "Desert Bark" flagstone steps connect levels of the gar-den and edge the pea-gravel paths. Les designed and built two handsome redwood footbridges to span a dry streambed that "flows" between the paths.

Patrick's goal was to plant a wide variety of desert-climate plants in a lush style that he calls a "dry jungle." There is an

ABOVE LEFT: Patrick's vintage Bauer pottery, including the turquoise and burnt orange pieces grouped here, were inspired by the weather and lifestyles of Southern California. Displayed on a glass-topped side table, the still life is a gathering of succulent plants and just-picked limes contained in Bauer saucers and flowerpots.
RIGHT: Patrick's deft placement of several golden barrel cactus plants (*Echinocactus grusonii*) lends a visual rhythm to the landscape. Resembling thorny tuffets, the spherical cactuses are native to the American Southwest and Mexico. When these tough plants are backlit by the setting sun, each rib, spine, and thorn is shown in detailed relief.

ABOVE: A burnished aluminum sculpture, paired with metallic-looking specimens of *Agave guiengola*, lends an exciting and graphic feeling to the landscape. Titled *Ventana,* the contemporary seven-foot piece was fabricated by local Fallbrook artist Peter Mitten.

DESIGN
ARCHITECTURE: Patrick Anderson

LANDSCAPE: Patrick Anderson

emphasis on aloes (he grows more than two hundred varieties of the fleshy, clumping plant, known for its intense orange, yellow, and red winter blooms that emerge up to 3 feet tall). Against the pointed blue green stems, these brilliant flowers remind visitors that there's nothing dull about the desert floral palette. Dozens of agaves, the alien-looking century plants, have ominous spikes and thorns, adding structure and form to the landscape.

These architectural plants show up in bold relief against the golden dining pavilion. Like Patrick and Les's house, the pavilion was originally finished in white stucco. But when the house needed repainting a few years ago, Patrick decided it was time to experiment with color. "I got really bored with white," he admits. "I thought about salmon and terra-cotta. But ultimately, I liked the idea of a Tuscan gold." Patrick worked with his friend Alan Richards, whom he calls a "color guru," to test at least ten shades of gold. "We wanted it bright but not garish, dark but not oppressive. One was too mustardy. One was school bus yellow. Another, too buttercup," Patrick recalls. "Finally we found the perfect one. The paint chip name was Golden Retriever."

Patrick and Les, both dog lovers, thought this aptly named

paint color was the perfect hue, although they lightened the mixture one shade to mellow its intensity. A simple coat of golden paint, reminiscent of ocher, has infused the property with much-needed warmth, Patrick admits. "The new finish has helped the pavilion settle into the landscape. Maroon, purple, and scarlet plants "sing against the golden pavilion," he adds.

The sunny palette that appears in Patrick's planting schemes is equally present in his collection of Bauer pottery. "I'm particularly fond of how the gold pavilion looks with my turquoise pottery," Patrick says.

Each January, Patrick and Les host a garden party—Sweets, Savories, and Succulents—for their friends to coincide with the aloe blooming season. A celebration of the winter garden in its splendor, it gives fellow plant fanatics a chance to enjoy an afternoon in this alluring desert landscape. "It's absolutely beautiful," Patrick says. Indeed, he has conjured up an otherworldly—and exquisite—place where people and plants appear equally content.

MATERIALS
ROOF: Mission-style terra-cotta tiles with terra-cotta finial

EXTERIOR: painted stucco

FLOOR: cement tile

SOUTHERN COMFORT

THREE GENERATIONS OF THE LYLE FAMILY ENJOY A 12-ACRE PLAYGROUND IN RURAL GEORGIA. THE GROUNDS ARE POPULATED WITH GARDEN HIDEAWAYS FOR ENTERTAINMENT, RELAXATION, COLLECTIONS, AND EVEN A HISTORY LESSON.

Brenda and Gerald Lyle collect and display relics of their southern heritage, including two cabins from the 1830s.

ABOVE: An oval garden window in the latticework folly. OPPOSITE: The folly stands at the center of an exuberant scheme formed by four 10-by-15-foot perennial beds. Brenda credits perennial expert Angie Moore and landscape designer Kathy Montgomery for inspiring her passion for plants.

About 35 miles west of Atlanta in Douglas County sits a 12-acre wooded property simply known as "the Farm." Here, Brenda and Gerald Lyle embrace the country life and all of its charms. High school sweethearts who grew up in Cobb County, outside Atlanta, the couple has been married for forty-four years. They raised two children, who live nearby with their families, including four young grandchildren.

In the mid-1970s, after residing in South Carolina for several years, they returned to Georgia when Gerald, a sales executive for a carpet manufacturer, was relocated to Atlanta. Their son, Shane, and daughter, Stella, were both under the age of ten, and the Lyles wanted to raise them beyond the suburbs.

MISSION
To give heart and soul to a country property and its distinct places for retreat, reflection, and creative expression

MUST-HAVES
Each of their backyard getaways tells a chapter in Lyle narrative: The retreat acts as a stand-alone family room; the folly is an open-air destination in a lavish perennial garden; the collections-filled garden room belies its origins as a chicken house; and two historic cabins inspire grandchildren with stories of the past.

INSPIRATION
A sentimental love of historic buildings, country antiques, and humble, timeworn artifacts

DESIGN CHALLENGES
To give each structure its distinct place in the larger landscape

CREATIVE SOLUTIONS
Eye-catching scenes were created to capture a moment in time, tell a story, and establish a purpose for Brenda and Gerald's unique "sheds."

ABOVE LEFT: The retreat's exposed-beam interior, wood-paneled walls, antique fireplace mantle, and sporting collections lend a lodge-like feeling to the room. RIGHT: Inside her 16-by-16-foot "Garden Room," which once housed poultry, Brenda displays her myriad collections of early American antiques in creative ways. An old metal gate frames a seasonal wreath; a vintage game board is artfully hung; a goldfish bowl now contains glass flower frogs.

PREVIOUS PAGE: Candlelight and lanterns cast a toasty glow on a summer evening where Brenda has set the patio table for hors d'oeuvres. The overhead pergola forms an open-air roof to connect the dining room (not seen) with "the Retreat," a stand-alone family room seen through a bank of French doors.

They discovered a 1960s farmhouse with pastures and a wooded area populated by native oaks and hickory trees. "When we moved here, it was on a dirt road," Brenda recalls. "It was very much the country and we liked that."

The "charm" she and Gerald saw included an original chicken house, probably dating to the 1940s. Prior owners had kept more than four thousand poultry, and later cattle, in the long, narrow structure. Despite its humble origins, Brenda loved the property. "We saw a lot of potential," she confides.

Brenda didn't become an avid gardener until her late forties. That was also when she began working full-time, helping to run Strathmore Floors, the Atlanta-based business the Lyles started in 1993 with their son, Shane. Until then the "garden" had always been a large vegetable patch located between their house and the pasture.

Where the vegetable garden once flourished now stands a perennial garden worthy of the English countryside. Carefree clumps of nostalgic favorites—phlox, daisies, daylilies, black-eyed Susan, verbena, and crocosmia—thrive in four 10-by-15-foot quadrants that form the design. Emerging above the cheerful flower heads is Brenda and Gerald's collection of whimsical birdhouses. At the heart of this garden is the "folly," a lattice pergola with a vine-covered peaked roof. As the perennials matured, they soon dwarfed the diminutive gazebo, originally built as an 8-foot square structure with swings at both ends.

The Lyles extended and enclosed the ends, using 2-by-6-inch and 2-by-8-inch boards to lend stature and triple the size. They bumped up the roof, adding a cupola and a weather vane. "Windows" in the sides and on the ends are formed by fetching oval openings, providing those seated inside picture-perfect views across the property. A rock floor and furnishings create a solid, roomlike feeling for the space, while a quiet pool of water at the center reminds them this is a setting inspired by nature's beauty.

Brenda's love of antiques blends nicely with her interest in gardening, evidenced by the many collections she displays in her "Garden Room." From the tarnished to the refined, her

"When we have a party, we open the retreat doors and the dining room doors— and it's a wonderful space."

—BRENDA LYLE

BELOW LEFT: Brenda lined the walls of the "Garden Room" with green bead board and hung vintage birdcages from brackets. RIGHT: Songbirds now reside in the ornamental yet functional birdhouses in the perennial garden.

RIGHT: Covered by a pergola, the 16-by-24-foot brick patio links the dining room and retreat and serves as an outdoor entertaining area. BELOW: Furnished with weatherproof wicker, the garden folly has a stone floor and oval openings through which to admire the plantings.

OPPOSITE: The Lyles acquired two circa 1830s cabins and restored them beneath a stand of hickory and oak trees. The one-room log structure at left was once owned by Cherokee Indians; the slightly larger cabin probably housed early Georgia settlers. They rebuilt the stone chimney, connected the two structures with a covered porch, and furnished interiors true to the period.

OWNERS
Brenda and Gerald Lyle

DESIGN
ARCHITECTURE: Brenda and Gerald Lyle

CONSTRUCTION: Strathmore Floors—Design – Cabinets

LANDSCAPE: Kathy Montgomery

objects are gathered in a 16-by-16-foot portion of the chicken house. With its separate entrance and large-paned window, the space feels like a country cottage. The interior walls are finished in bead board painted the color of vintage jadeite glass. Brenda covered the floor in a durable sea grass and upholstered ticking-striped cushions for her set of weathered wicker, which was brought indoors after spending years in the garden.

This room is designed around a floral and botanical theme. One shelf contains a collection of "five finger" flower vases, many from Gerald's family. A green hutch displays yellowware, milk glass, transferware, and pottery organized by color. Early-twentieth-century garden books are stacked on a dry sink, sharing the scene with vintage flower frogs. Antique birdcages hang from wall brackets and a grouping of miniature garden furniture is arranged on a side table.

The transformation from humble shack to gracious, feminine chamber is one that Brenda loves sharing with her friends. "We once had a dirt floor, with the hoses and rakes in here. Now I have my collections and wicker."

Six years ago, after first considering a home addition, Gerald and Brenda instead decided to build a freestanding retreat. They needed more space but wanted it to be separate from the main living area.

Built to resemble their farmhouse—with the same

peaked roofline, shingle siding, and black shutters and doors—the room they call "the Retreat" measures less than 400 square feet. Its orientation mirrors the back of the Lyles' house, where the dining room windows once overlooked a prosaic area of the garden. Now the house and retreat display a bank of French doors linked by a 16-by-24-foot pergola-covered brick patio. The patio creates an outdoor dining room, giving Brenda twice the entertaining space she used to have.

"When we have a party, we open the retreat doors and the dining room doors—and it's a wonderful space," she enthuses. When the weather is pleasant, gatherings flow seamlessly from indoors to outdoors. Candles on the rust-covered chandelier are lit, music plays on outdoor speakers, and guests enjoy coffee and dessert in front of a fireplace inside the retreat. "We sit out there to talk and just enjoy one another's company," Brenda says. "It gives us a place to get away without leaving home."

The interior echoes their home, including rough-cut beams, wood-paneled walls, a basket-weave brick floor, and a vintage fireplace mantel. The lodge-style decor imparts a casual elegance created by antiques and collections reflecting the sporting life.

"So many people who come here think this was the original kitchen to the house, and I hate to disappoint them," Brenda confides. "They think it has always been here."

MATERIALS

The Folly

ROOF/WALLS: 2-by-6-inch, 2-by-8-inch, and 1-by-1-inch latticework painted white; copper dome cupola and weather vane

FLOOR: sand-set Tennessee fieldstone

The Garden Room

ROOF: tin (original)

EXTERIOR: board siding (original) painted barn red

CEILING: smooth plywood painted dark green

WALLS: bead board painted green

WINDOWS: double-hung, divided cottage-style, painted white

DOOR: 12-pane French doors painted black

FLOOR: woven sea grass carpeting

The Retreat

ROOF: composite roof tile

EXTERIOR: cedar shingles painted barn red

CEILING: tongue-and-groove wood

WALLS: wide-plank wood paneling

WINDOWS: double-hung, 18-pane (2 sets); interior stained brown; exterior painted black

DOORS: four 15-pane French doors painted black: two stationary, two operable

FLOOR: basket-weave laid brick

COTTAGE COURTYARD

LIKE A SECRET GARDEN ROOM, A TINY ENCLOSURE CONTAINS PLANTS AND ANTIQUES ARTFULLY DISPLAYED FOR THE DELIGHT OF ITS OWNER AND HER GUESTS

Paved in red tile, the garden-inspired courtyard with vine-covered walls serves as an intimate and enchanting transition between Lani and Larry Freymiller's house and garage.

ABOVE: The metal tines of a weathered garden rake (its handle long since lost) serve as a tool organizer for Lani Freymiller's trowels and cultivators.
OPPOSITE: A dense "wall" of creeping fig cushions the weathered stucco while variegated ivy spreads over the wicker-topped table. Lani designed the courtyard using comfortable roomlike finishes, including French Provençal print pillows and an iron armchair.
FOLLOWING PAGE: An original cottage door opens to reveal the rustic room that was once used for hanging laundry and later as a greenhouse. After a falling branch destroyed its roof, Lani and Larry converted the small space into a charming courtyard.

Lani and Larry Freymiller bought their California ranch house in 1974, when Rancho Santa Fe was still a remote village of eucalyptus groves. They used the 10-by-16-foot wedge-shaped room adjacent to the garage for hanging laundry on a clothesline suspended between two walls. After Lani gave Larry a yellow cymbidium for Christmas, the couple enclosed the space with a glass roof to create a greenhouse for Larry's burgeoning orchid collection (the laundry room was moved indoors). But when a storm knocked a branch of an aging eucalyptus tree through the roof, they decided to leave the space open to the sky. "It had an ancient look—like our own Roman ruin," Lani jokes.

MISSION
To salvage the remains of an orchid house after a eucalyptus branch crashed through its glass roof

MUST-HAVES
Comfortable seating for two, display tables for potted plants, a pair of vintage shutters to mimic a window

INSPIRATION
An aging courtyard in the south of France or Italy

DESIGN CHALLENGES
Lani wanted to invite light into the courtyard and soften the bare appearance of the solid white stucco walls. She also hoped to disguise the plastic water cisterns installed at one end of the space.

CREATIVE SOLUTIONS
A quartet of vintage leaded windows occupies a once bleak wall and makes the space more roomlike. Nearly every surface of stucco and wood is now covered with *Ficus pumila* (creeping fig), an evergreen vine that creates a delicate tracery of oval leaves. The water system is hidden behind a picket "wall." "The fencing gives me another surface for hanging art and plants," Lani says.

ABOVE LEFT: Twin privets on standards create a formal display against a wall of picket fencing (it also hides plastic cisterns). A thrift-shop oil painting is hung here in all but rainy weather. RIGHT: Spilling water from a cast-stone wall fountain lends a quiet melody to the courtyard.

OPPOSITE, LEFT: Lani placed a vintage workbench against one wall, topping it with an oversize mirror, pottery, ancient wine jugs, and potted plants. "I decorate it just like I'm getting ready for a dinner party," she says. RIGHT: Just-harvested perennials and herbs fill a market basket that hangs in the doorway.

Mother Nature is to blame for a laundry room's evolution from orchid house to storybook garden courtyard. For Lani and Larry, the once utilitarian space is now a tranquil entry to their home, furnished with timeworn benches, a tribal rug, and potted plants. "At first, we didn't want people to go to our back door," Lani confides. "But now the front door rarely gets used—and everybody comes through the courtyard."

High school sweethearts who grew up in La Mesa, about twenty-five miles east of San Diego, Lani and Larry have embraced the rural nature of Rancho Santa Fe. The area was established in the late 1800s when the Santa Fe Railroad Company planted eucalyptus groves to produce railroad ties. "But they planted the wrong species—this type of eucalyptus loses its outer camber, so the trees began to split," Lani points out. "The railroad company eventually abandoned these groves."

Real estate speculators acquired 6,200 acres by 1927 and developed the community of Rancho Santa Fe. Designed by Lilian Jenette Rice, one of the first women to attend architec-

ture school at Berkeley, the area has grown and expanded from an isolated community to a suburb of San Diego, though Lani insists, "It still has that remote charm."

After living near the Pacific Ocean in Del Mar, where "we thought we'd be forever," Lani and Larry explored Rancho Santa Fe at the urging of some friends. "That was thirty-four years ago. We walked in the front door of this California ranch and that was it," she recalls.

The couple has added several personal touches to the house, including an upstairs master suite, a family room, and several outdoor patios. They first used the open-air 10-by-16-foot space between the house and garage for hanging laundry. It was a serviceable spot hidden behind a stucco wall and accessed through a kitchen door.

Then Larry, who is a dentist, discovered the joy of growing orchids.

"I remember giving Larry a huge yellow cymbidium for Christmas, and he became interested in growing more of them,"

"When people come through on garden tours, they enter this space and don't want to leave."

—LANI FREYMILLER

ABOVE: Lani's preference for symmetry is revealed in this vignette. Her sets of recycled shutters, iron flowerpot brackets and shrub-filled pots mirror one another on opposite sides of the urn in the center.

OWNERS
Lani and Larry Freymiller

DESIGN
INTERIOR: Lani Freymiller

Lani, a retired elementary schoolteacher, recalls. "We realized we could enclose the laundry space, add a door, heater, and fan, and Larry could raise orchids to his heart's content."

They asked a friend to install four vintage leaded windows in one of the solid walls. The windows brightened the room and created architectural interest when viewed from an adjacent patio. Overhead, a roof of chicken wire–embedded glass protected the light-loving tropical plants from cool winter temperatures.

While Larry grew orchids, Lani tended to the rest of their 2½-acre garden. Lani's design philosophy has evolved over time. She recalls wanting a carefree garden filled with herbs and roses twenty years ago. "I couldn't think of going anywhere beyond the chaos of high color, fresh flowers, and primitive plantings. I remember saying that I could never enjoy a symmetrical garden." But the trees have continued to block out sunnier spots in the landscape, and Lani has in turn embraced the quiet formality of a shade garden. Evergreen shrubs, including boxwood, myrtle, euonymus, and pittosporum, occupy large containers, variegated ivies trail from flowerpots, and vibrant green hostas populate the garden. She grows hydrangeas, which are harvested for huge bouquets, and ferns, which fill urns or adorn the edges of paths.

In 1995, a storm downed several branches of an aging eucalyptus tree, and one shattered the glass roof of Larry's orchid house. "That storm just made us appreciate the strength of the eucalyptus trees so close to our house, and we decided not to replace the glass," Lani points out.

But what to do with the ruins of the orchid room? "It kind of reminded us of an old house in the south of France or Italy," she recalls.

LEFT: Although it is without a roof, the courtyard reveals itself as an intimate room with leaded windows, a tribal rug on the red tile floor, and colorful textiles. Café chairs and a small table accommodate two for afternoon tea.

ABOVE: Lani and Larry recruited a friend to mount vintage windows into the stucco wall. Creeping fig has partially obscured the frames, although there is still space for flowerpots on the windowsills.

The aging red tile floor and stucco walls were salvageable. Most of the room's surfaces were by then covered in creeping fig. What the space needed was a makeover, and Lani filled it with "all the essentials—a mirror, table, chairs, and plants." Motivated by the serendipitous nature of antiquing, Lani began to collect pieces that could withstand exposure to the elements. From her point of view, the more the top of a wood table was buckling or paint was chipped on a bench, the better. She salvaged and hung weathered shutters to create the appearance of a window against a vine-covered wall, adding brackets to display potted ivy topiaries.

A set of wire bistro chairs flanks a wicker-topped table, which is just large enough for sharing tea with a girlfriend. "I like that one-on-one time; this room is ideal for that," she says. A Dutch door opens from her kitchen onto the courtyard, allowing Lani to serve drinks, coffee, or sandwiches easily.

She considers the courtyard a bridge between her house and garden. "This has the intimacy of a home, because it allows me to bring the indoors outside."

MATERIALS

WALLS: white st ucco

WINDOWS: vintage leaded glass

DOOR: original to house

FLOOR: Mexican terra-cotta tile

POETIC LICENSE

USING A SEPIA-TONED PALETTE AND TERRA-COTTA ACCENTS, AN ARTIST DEIGNER DREAMS UP A RESTFUL ENCLOSURE

ABOVE: Shirley Alexandra Watts melded fourteenth-century Italian poetry with twenty-first-century billboard text to create a private, meditative space where water and sky meet. Eight-inch-square Italian terra-cotta tiles, installed upside down to reveal a grooved pattern, form the floor. The traditional urn-shaped fountain is displayed behind a cube of modern Plexiglas onto which Shirley etched poetry lines. Translated they read "clear, fresh, and sweet water."

Shirley Alexandra Watts, a Bay Area artist and garden designer, loves the hand-thrown urns, bowls, and saucers crafted by the Sicilian potter Carmelo Milone. To showcase the vessels, she partnered with Lou Truesdell of American Soil & Stone Products based in Richmond, California, who imports the Sicilian pottery. Her concept: to construct an inventive four-sided outdoor "pavilion" in the heart of an industrial stone yard. Shirley used decidedly modern materials to create the structure, including square steel bars, recycled billboard panels, hollow-core doors, and garage hardware. Together, these parts form an 11-foot-square "cube" with abstract panels for walls and no ceiling. "It's a meditative, 'roofless' room," she explains.

It's no surprise that a landscape designer trained in painting and sculpture would break with traditional ideas of what constitutes a "garden shelter." Shirley's installations range from two award-winning gardens at the San Francisco Flower and Garden Show to Hortus Contemplationis, a companion garden to a still-life exhibit at the San Jose Museum of Art.

The idea of creating a roofless garden shelter germinated while she designed the museum garden, Shirley says. "I had this space on the second floor that you reach by going through the galleries. It was surrounded on three sides by the building and it had one wall of windows, but there was no ceiling."

When entering the courtyard-like space she was moved by the powerful sensation of "sky actually penetrating the building," and by watching how museumgoers responded to the presence of sun, clouds, and sky. "As soon as you have four walls, your gaze goes up and you become more aware of the sky," Shirley observes. She began to play with concepts for a freestanding garden structure with sliding doors. "I liked the idea that you could close this whole thing off and be inside this little box, where everything else was outside."

"I am very interested in what happens when you enter a space like this and close all the doors. You become aware of the sky, which is a huge part of our landscape."

LEFT: The 11-foot-square room has no ceiling and was built using a framework of 2-inch-square steel bars bolted at the corners. Portions of Greek-style lettering and fragments of larger-than-life eyes, noses, and mouths from a promotional billboard are reassembled like a collage, covering sixteen hanging doors that slide open or closed.

BELOW: The Sicilian pottery and a curved concrete bench that Shirley also designed present a restful still life.

Shirley created a bubbling central water feature using a traditional stone urn mounted on a recycled brake drum "pedestal." The fountain is sheathed by a 30-inch-square cube of Plexiglas, which reveals a silhouette of the urn inside. "I wanted to play with light and translucency," she explains. But the box needed some text, and Shirley searched for the ideal piece of Italian poetry to etch on the cube's surface. She sent a photograph of the project to Fulvia Varaschini, a friend from her years as a postgraduate art student in Rome, and asked for help.

"She gave me the opening line of *Canzoniere 126*, a poem by Francesco Petrarca," Shirley says. It reads: *Chiare, fresche et dolci acque*. The translation of the fourteenth-century phrase is pure and appealing: clear, fresh and sweet water. "Once I read the entire poem, I realized it takes place in a garden setting."

CREEK HOUSE

ENCLOSED BY GLASS AND SCREENS, A RUSTIC
"ROOM IN THE WOODS" GIVES A NORTHWEST COUPLE
A COOL, RESTFUL VANTAGE POINT FOR
WATCHING BIRDS AND WILDLIFE

After restoring the banks of Silver Creek, which runs through their

7-acre property in the northwest corner of Washington State,

Terry and Dave Maczuga added a small, secluded structure nearby.

ABOVE: A Tibetan prayer flag lends color and movement to the mostly green setting. OPPOSITE: As Terry and Dave Maczuga restored the banks of Silver Creek, a stream running through their 7-acre property that had been overgrown with blackberries, they dreamed up a small but elegant shelter from which to enjoy views of the water, cooler temperatures, returning native plants, and resident wildlife. Measuring nearly 120 square feet, the Creek House is a result of their ideas and their hands-on construction efforts.

What Terry Maczuga jokingly calls "a mosquito shelter" is actually one of the most inviting and tranquil destinations at Silver Creek Gardens, the 7-acre Bellingham, Washington, property that she and her husband, Dave, call home.

Dave and Terry devised a trail system through their land that takes about a half hour to navigate. You begin at their house and stroll toward the small spring-fed creek, about 800 feet away at the bottom of a ravine. The lawn and ornamental gardens give way to a meadow path mown through an orchard. It connects with a needle-strewn walkway that descends toward the woods below. As you approach this shady area, which borders Silver Creek, the temperature is noticeably cooler. The atmosphere is quiet, almost reverent.

MISSION
To create a woodland getaway using salvaged building materials

MUST-HAVES
A small, noninvasive footprint that wouldn't require a building permit; glass walls, screened windows, and a porchlike entry; an interior that accommodates a table and comfortable seating

INSPIRATION
A bug-free place where two nature lovers can observe and enjoy their native woodland and listen to water splashing through the creek

DESIGN CHALLENGES
To build a freestanding shelter that is aesthetically pleasing and sustainable

CREATIVE SOLUTIONS
Terry and Dave used "odds and ends" and recycled materials accumulated from prior home improvement projects, including yellow cedar from an old deck, aging fence boards, and double-paned windows salvaged from the sunroom.

ABOVE LEFT: Simple pleasures are fitting for the screened and windowed room, including Terry's flower arrangement using two natives, wild mock orange (*Philadelphus lewisii*) and western spirea (*Spiraea douglasii*), and glasses of amber-hued hard cider, brewed each year after apple harvest.
RIGHT: The orange-streaked feather left by a resident flicker is tucked between the wall studs.

PREVIOUS PAGE: Austere but comfortable, the furnishings accommodate two for bird watching, book reading, or a refreshing drink on a hot summer day. Built by Dave Maczuga and an artist-carpenter friend with mostly salvaged materials, the Creek House is appealing for its earthy materials and excellent craftsmanship.

Partially visible between the trunks of Douglas firs and Western red cedars stands a modest but inviting structure. Constructed in wood and glass, with shutterlike coverings that open to reveal screened panels, the lichen-colored building is just shy of 120 square feet. Upon entering, calm descends on its occupants. It's easy to stay silent here or perhaps speak in whispers, because you feel like a guest observer of nature in all its glory. With the right tools—a pair of binoculars and a field guide to Northwest birds—it's possible to spot a nuthatch fly by or study a wren resting on a branch. "We love to come here with a bottle of hard cider or a glass of wine and sit down to enjoy the birds," Dave says.

The Maczugas' rural property in Bellingham, Washington, about 30 miles from the British Columbia border, was once pastureland. Terry moved there in 1981 with her first husband and a new baby. Terry's life suddenly changed two years later, after having built their house and planted a small garden: her husband was killed in a fishing accident, and she found herself a young, single mother with a toddler.

Hanging on to the property was important to Terry, who taught middle-school science for several years before starting work on an MA in teaching. While in graduate school, she took a part-time job at Cloud Mountain Farm, a specialty nursery in nearby Everson, known for growing and stocking high-quality fruit-bearing and ornamental trees and shrubs. She eventually abandoned the prospect of writing a thesis for a career in horticulture.

In 1992, she met Dave Maczuga, a geologist who had come to the Northwest from New Jersey in the early 1990s to take a position as a wetlands scientist. After marrying the following year, the couple collaborated on the ornamental garden near the house. Terry previously used most of the acreage to raise goats and sheep. Since the animals were gone, the area gave way to an ever-expanding lineup of trees and shrubs. "The garden kind of snowballed," Terry explains.

The couple also planted more than seventy fruit and nut trees in a separate pasture where cattle once grazed. By 2000, the trees were producing more than 500 pounds of fruit annually,

"People have that 'wow' reaction when they come over the ravine and see the Creek House. Everybody wants to go inside and sit down."

—TERRY MACZUGA

LEFT: After watching *Rivers and Tides*, a film about artist Andy Goldsworthy, Dave was inspired to weave his own Goldsworthyesque "nests" using downed cedar twigs gathered from the riverbank. Situated among native sword ferns (*Polystichum munitum*), the alluring circles measure 6 feet at their bases and taper to a small hole at the domes.

ABOVE: Terry (*left*) and Dave (*right*) explore their landscape via a system of trails that leads through cultivated and wild areas. They installed stepping-stone bridges and board crossings to continue the trail over Silver Creek.

OPPOSITE: Situated beneath western red cedar trees and built mostly from recycled wood and windows, the Maczugas' Creek House provides protection and shelter while remaining outdoors in the wooded ravine they love.

OWNER
Terry and Dave Maczuga

DESIGN
ARCHITECTURE: Dave Maczuga

CONSTRUCTION: Dave Maczuga and Ken Speer

LANDSCAPE: Terry and Dave Maczuga

prompting Terry and Dave to try brewing English-style hard cider. Two of their preferred apple varieties, 'Kingston Black' and 'Ashmead's Kernel', make a deliciously crisp golden liquid that tastes a bit like dry white wine. Distilled into simple brown bottles, their Silver Creek hard cider is a favorite among friends.

In addition to working with Terry to plant an orchard and ornamental gardens, Dave has spent more than a decade restoring the banks of Silver Creek with native vegetation. His first task was to eradicate wild blackberries that were choking the stream, which supports a run for native Coho salmon. "The only way to get rid of the blackberries is to mow them down and shade them out," Terry explains. Dave planted hemlocks and other Northwest conifers; he added fifty young vine maples and cottonwoods and relocated sword ferns from elsewhere on the property. He introduced native perennials, including Western bleeding heart (*Dicentra formosa*), coral bells (*Heuchera micrantha*), and false Solomon's seal (*Maianthemum racemosum*), which sparkle in the dappled light that streams through the evergreen canopy overhead.

Dave and Terry initially placed a few log benches here to enjoy sitting near the restored creek. "We noticed how much cooler it was in the ravine, but it was also very buggy," Terry says. "We kept thinking about finding a spot to build something here." Whatcom County's building codes restrict construction within 100 feet of the creek. Dave and Terry measured locations and found a possible site tucked beneath a few mature cedar trees. "We had to fit it to the site and we wanted to stay small enough so as not to require a permit," Terry explains. "Plus, we wanted to use materials we had on hand, so the design was also determined by the amount of glass we had."

In 2003, working with Ken Speer, a friend and an artist-carpenter, Dave set the footings for the "Creek House." The men used a mortise-and-tenon timber framing method, inserting windows recycled from a sunroom to create ceiling-to-floor glass walls on the sides. The building's corners are formed by screened panels for cross-ventilation; hinged wood "shutters" can be closed when temperatures drop. A low-pitched roof extends beyond the structure, partially sheltering an 18-inch-deep ledge that serves as a porch. Dave is pleased that he salvaged materials for the little structure, the completed size of which is less than the county's 120-square-foot maximum for a building without a permit. "Except for the door and the plywood base, everything is recycled," he says.

Dave and Terry's "sustainable" attitude is reflected in their stewardship of Silver Creek Gardens. Dave has woven fallen cedar twigs to create alluring Andy Goldsworthy–inspired sculptures. The couple has harvested their fruit for homemade blueberry wine and hard cider. They also have restored the creek with native plants and built a woodland retreat from recycled materials.

"As gas prices go up and it gets harder to justify traveling away, we don't feel like we need to leave," Terry says. "The whole philosophy behind the Creek House and the garden in general is that we can be happy staying here."

"I love being here and feeling like I'm away from everything."

—DAVE MACZUGA

MATERIALS

ROOF: rolled composite roofing and cedar duff

WALLS: salvaged double-paned windows framed with recycled wood

WINDOWS: recycled glass and screens

DOOR: fir-framed single-glass panel

FLOOR: recycled yellow cedar decking

SECOND ACT

AN INTERIOR DESIGNER BREATHES NEW LIFE INTO A 1930S HAMPTONS GARAGE, TURNING IT INTO A SERENE DESTINATION FOR WEEKEND VISITORS

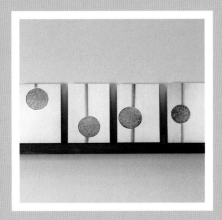

Where others saw "potting shed" Betty Wasserman saw "guesthouse."
She renovated the barn-shaped structure with her signature "country modern"
style, using furniture and art to create a cozy backyard getaway.

ABOVE: An untitled series by photographer Lisa Ross is arranged on a ledge. OPPOSITE: The 1930s garage gained new purpose as a guest cottage when Betty updated it with French doors, square windows, lighting, and a sophisticated interior. Its exterior color was influenced by the dark-stained farm buildings that stood in the Hamptons long before weekenders began coming here. Laid in a checkered pattern to create a patio and walkway, square paving stones enliven the lawn between Betty's home and guest cottage. PAGE 163: The original beams look rugged beneath an open ceiling.

When she eyed the 600-square-foot garage at the back of the half-acre Southampton lot, interior designer Betty Wasserman discovered a diamond in the rough. "It was shaped like a barn and I immediately saw it as an opportunity," she recalls. "I knew that I could do something with it." Betty loved the charm of its gambrel-style roof and small attached potting shed. Reimagining it as a guest cottage, she transformed the little building. It now gives Betty—and her weekend visitors—much-needed extra space. A new pair of horizontally divided French doors faces the garden. "I didn't want the doors and windows to be too modern," she notes. A hint of pale blue green in the creamy wall paint creates an overall calmness to the room.

MISSION
To transform an aging garage and potting shed into a guesthouse for overnight visitors without losing its vintage character

MUST-HAVES
Efficient space planning, built-in cabinets, and a Murphy bed, plus a studio kitchen and bath

INSPIRATION
Historic dark-stained Southampton farm buildings

DESIGN CHALLENGES
Making a dusty, unfinished garage with concrete floor and sliding barn doors look and feel comfortable for guests

CREATIVE SOLUTIONS
Custom French doors and cottage-style windows; the addition of insulation, electricity, and plumbing; a tiny but elegant bathroom and efficiency kitchen with storage; the reuse of two original barn doors as a nod to the past

ABOVE LEFT: Betty designed the custom maple bench with a small storage drawer. The piece is part of her bettyhome.com line of furniture and accessories. RIGHT: A desk made from weathered wood, also designed by Betty, stands in a windowed nook between two small closets. A pair of small oil paintings by Louise Crandell rests on the windowsill.

OPPOSITE, LEFT: The custom walnut credenza displays flowers and candles that reflect the vibrant brushstrokes in the untitled paintings by artist Melinda Stickney Gibson. RIGHT: Betty designed the door that disguises a Murphy bed by "weaving" walnut veneer strips over-and-under steel rods.

Betty selected chocolate brown stain for the exterior, inspired by a favorite local farm building. "The brown makes the barn a little quieter and recessed on the property," she points out. "The white windows and doors are highlighted against it."

Trained in fine art and business at Northeastern University in Boston, Betty knows how to size up a property's potential when she sees it: from New York apartments to a 75-acre New Jersey horse farm to vacation homes in the Bahamas. Her career has progressed from art consulting to interior, lighting, and furniture design.

Studying business and studio art made sense to Betty, although she admits her parents thought she was confused. "I simply thought I was diverse," she says. "I had no idea that the two disciplines would turn into a career." Betty knew she might not become a painter but she wanted an art-filled life. "I realized after my first semester that I was not nearly as talented as anyone in my class. But I knew that I understood art."

where alder trees and mountain hemlocks grow at its edge. "As you drive onto the property, or as you walk from the house to the field, you look through into a clearing, and there is this little chapel." Located about one hundred yards away from his house, Edgar appreciates the sense of "journey" required to reach it: he walks through a wooded area into the untended meadow to his peaceful chapel. Here, Edgar entertains guests for open-air cocktail parties, filling the chapel with dozens of candles at twilight for an intimate gathering.

BACKYARD ZEN

JAPANESE TRADITION WITH TEXAS-STYLE INFLUENCE
CREATES A BREEZY SUMMERHOUSE IN THE CITY

Eldon and Beverly Sutton gain new use for their sloped backyard with a

contemplative teahouse on "stilts" and an alluring two-level water feature.

ABOVE: A water iris reveals its pristine beauty. OPPOSITE: When Eldon and Beverly Sutton decided to add a teahouse to their Austin backyard, they wanted it "to look at home in Texas." Working with architect Gregory Thomas and landscape designer Fred Strauss, the couple suggested the structure approximate their dining room's dimensions. The resulting Texas-style teahouse utilizes post-and-beam, timber-framed construction, a standing-seam metal roof, and panoramic views of the Sutton's wooded ravine. Ten-by-ten-inch posts support the graceful building and accommodate the sloped lot. FOLLOWING PAGE: Tongue-and-groove cedar comprises the "ceremonial wall."

"Beverly always imagined she wanted a teahouse, but I think we should call it a Gin House, because it's used for enjoying gin on ice at evening cocktails."

—ELDON SUTTON

Eldon and Beverly Sutton envisioned a teahouse that blended Asian and Texan architectural styles and related to their all-American home and garden. Like many inspired design solutions, the idea emerged organically, as clients and designers discussed wants, needs, and options. "It started out very simply," Beverly acknowledges. "I wanted to be able to sit outside—without bugs."

After learning of Eldon's several trips to Japan for academic meetings and of Beverly's collection of Japanese prints and woodblocks, the design team suggested a screened pavilion reminiscent of a Japanese teahouse.

MISSION
To fashion a garden structure that separates humans from insects and provides its occupants a refreshing and peaceful place in the landscape

MUST-HAVES
Architectural detailing, post-and-beam construction, standing-seam metal roof to protect interior from sun and rain, bug-proof screened walls and door, ceiling fan

INSPIRATION
Japanese teahouse with Texas flavor

DESIGN CHALLENGES
A crumbling retaining wall at the edge of a ravine rendered much of the landscape unsuitable for building. The owners envisioned a backyard Asian-style teahouse but wanted the design to look relevant in context with their 1940s brick-and-wood home.

CREATIVE SOLUTIONS
Teahouse touches (such as a deep overhanging roof and a ceremonial wall) and an interior made spacious with transparent panels of window screening import an Asian feel. The 10-by-13-foot building rests on 5-foot posts, creating a level structure that appears to float above the sloping property.

"We're perfectly aware that we have things to do indoors, but it's hard to stop being here."

—BEVERLY SUTTON

Academics who have been married for forty-five years, Beverly and Eldon moved to Austin in the early 1960s. Their traditional, two-story Texas limestone house, built in the 1940s, accommodated the couple and two young daughters; over time, successive renovations—to add a garage, a bedroom, and a study—were finished in wood clapboard exterior siding.

The family's one-acre lot includes part of a wooded ravine. They enjoy having a bit of "wildness" in the midst of the city, listening to the pleasant clicking sound made by the wind blowing through the leaves of cottonwood trees. They fondly remember their daughters (now adults) playing on well-worn trails that led to Shoal Creek at the bottom of the property. The girls occasionally found horseshoes and square-head nails dating to the late 1800s when wagons and buggies traveled along the creek's edge. "This was considered worthless land, because it was hard to bring horses up the hill," recalls Eldon, a geneticist and the Ashbel Smith Professor Emeritus at the University of Texas.

For years, Beverly, a pediatrician and a child psychiatrist who teaches residents at Shoal Creek Hospital, rarely ventured outdoors because she hated the swarms of bugs common to Texas summers. Instead, she observed nature through the picture windows of the family room.

In 2004, the Suttons asked Fred Strauss, the owner of Thrive/Inside-Out, an Austin-based landscape business, to help them redesign the backyard. He tapped Gregory Thomas, an Austin architect and garden designer, to collaborate with him on the project.

"When Beverly mentioned the problem of bugs, I thought it would be nice if she could have a screened garden structure," Strauss recalls. Eldon asked for something that felt at home in Texas rather than Kyoto.

The differences between traditional Japanese architecture and a Texas-inspired version are subtle. Thomas and Strauss infused American sensibility into the teahouse design, making

OPPOSITE, LEFT: When enjoying drinks with friends, the Suttons hear the pleasant trickle of water dripping from pipes into two limestone-clad circular pools, one of which appears here. CENTER: Three of the 130-square-foot structure's walls are formed by fiberglass-screened panels to give Eldon and Beverly a bug-free environment from which to enjoy their garden. Builders also installed screening underneath the *Ipe* decking to keep insects from slipping through the tiny spaces.

ABOVE: *Hands on Hip,* a bronze figure by Kansas City–based sculptor Jim Corbin, stands at the terminus of the main path.

OWNERS
Eldon and Beverly Sutton

DESIGN
ARCHITECT: Gregory Thomas, CG&S Design-Build

CONTRACTOR: David Wilkes and Philip Perry, Trinity Builders

LANDSCAPE: Fred Strauss, Thrive/Inside-Out

it fit comfortably in Austin while hinting at its Eastern counterparts.

With post-and-beam, timber-framed construction similar to Japanese architecture, the 130-square-foot Western red cedar building perches on massive stilts. Ten-by-ten-inch posts provide support and they step down to accommodate the slope. The teahouse seemingly "floats" above the natural greenbelt, where branches from leafy Texas red oaks and elm trees allow dappled light to illuminate the yard.

Eldon and Beverly take a leisurely walk to the teahouse via two routes: either along a narrow *Ipe* boardwalk or over evenly spaced stepping-stones, which Thomas likens to crossing a moat. This idea pleases them, as it does their architect. "We wanted to give them choices in order to make the teahouse feel like an important destination," Thomas explains. "You don't hurry there. You need to go with a purpose in mind. It's both a physical and a psychological choice."

After practicing medicine for fifty years, Beverly jokes that she has tried to retire three times, but has yet to stop seeing patients or training medical students. In contrast, Eldon deadpans: "I know how to retire." Yet with their varied schedules, on weekend mornings or weekday evenings, from springtime to early winter, they often venture to the teahouse. "We're secluded here. It is pleasant and private and we hear the water running," Beverly says. "We're perfectly aware that we have things to do indoors, but it's hard to stop being here."

MATERIALS

ROOF: standing-seam metal roof

EXTERIOR: post-and-beam, timber-framed with cable detailing

INTERIOR WALLS: tongue-and-groove cedar on east-facing wall

WINDOWS: fiberglass screened paneling on three walls

DOOR: swinging screens

FLOOR: *Ipe* decking

OPPOSITE, TOP: Married forty-five years, Beverly, a pediatrician and child psychiatrist, and Eldon, a geneticist and University of Texas professor emeritus, often spend their free time relaxing in their garden. During Austin's buggy summer months, they move inside the teahouse. BOTTOM: "Where this building sits on the land and relates to the sun is part of its beauty," explains architect Gregory Thomas. He and landscaper Fred Strauss devised twin circle-in-a-square ponds that step down toward the edge of the garden to infuse water into the Asian-inspired Austin setting. Eldon and Beverly arrive at the teahouse by crossing the stepping-stone bridge or journeying along an *Ipe* boardwalk.

PLAY'S THE THING

"This place is one where children and animals can go in and out with reckless abandon. It may be a guesthouse someday, but for now, it's a playhouse."

—CAROL HICKS BOLTON

The best backyard escapades begin with a place that children (or grown-ups) can call their own. Detached from everyday routine, they are playful and frivolous destinations—the setting for kids' fantasies or for adults wishing to relive favorite childhood moments in a secret fort or hideout. Their designs are easygoing and unpretentious, intended to bring out the child in anyone.

Where better to experience physical or symbolic "escape" than in a separate place where laughter, daydreaming, and imagination are nurtured?

The playhouse-shed may be outfitted with a loft, a window seat, or a covered porch—or even a water-filled moat for dangling one's toes. There's a covert element, as its occupants disappear into their own world. It's the perfect setting for impromptu theatrical productions, afternoon tea, or a nocturnal party for friends. Design choices are adaptable, allowing the structure's use to change as a family grows. Durable, pet-friendly features are a plus. Laughter is required.

MOD POD

PLANT CONSERVATORY MEETS POOL PARTY WHEN A BROTHER-AND-SISTER TEAM DESIGNS A STEEL-FRAMED BACKYARD SHED

Loretta Fischer wanted a greenhouse to store her tropical plants during the winter months. When she asked her brother Harrison Bates to build it, the project quickly changed from ordinary to outrageous.

ABOVE: Loretta's landscape design philosophy eschews English-style perennials for bold, linear forms like horsetail (*Equisetum hyemale*). OPPOSITE: When Terrill and Loretta Fischer asked Harrison Bates, her brother, to design and build a backyard greenhouse, he brought a modern attitude to the task. The finished architecture uses ordinary greenhouse materials in an extraordinary manner, infusing the landscape with dramatic geometry and translucent light. When illuminated at dusk, the angular structure glows in silhouette, revealing striking outlines of tropical plants within. PAGE 183: Dashes of orange jazz up the vibrant blue tile flooring.

In Loretta Fischer's hands, creativity has taken many forms, from edible sweets to eye-pleasing landscapes. For ten years, this perky professional cook operated Loretta's Fabulous Cheesecakes of Texas, a bakery with two Austin locations. By 1995, after she met and married her husband, Terrill Fischer, a stand-up comic and real estate broker, Loretta sold the cheesecake business and began developing her own backyard. Today, she operates a landscape design firm, aptly named Hot Garden.

"Most people in Texas don't spend time in their yards when the weather gets hot, but I can sit here with my feet in the water and read while the sun goes down."

—LORETTA FISCHER

MISSION
To design a playful structure with dual uses—to store plants, tools, and bicycles and add splash to warm summer parties

MUST-HAVES
Polycarbonate greenhouse siding and roof, sliding doors and windows, and colorful lino tile flooring

INSPIRATION
A sculptural twist on build-it-yourself greenhouse kits

DESIGN CHALLENGES
Making a rectilinear shape more interesting; hiding exposed, unattractive footings at one edge of the structure where the grade changes

CREATIVE SOLUTIONS
Harrison Bates began with scale drawings of 7-foot squares. He cut them into triangles and by playing around with the shapes came up with an asymmetrical V-shaped structure topped with slanted rooflines. A bonus: the shallow, pentagon-shaped water feature that doubles as a tiny pool.

Like many city residents, Loretta and Terrill Fischer lacked space. After ten years together, they had maxed out a two-bedroom, one-bath 1940s ranch house measuring less than 1,000 square feet. In fact, Loretta needed the attached garage not for parking her car but for storing garden tools and dozens of potted tropical plants requiring winter shelter. That arrangement worked until 2001, when Terrill decided to have Loretta's brother Harrison Bates renovate the garage as his office, and Loretta's plants needed a new home.

During the garage redo, Loretta asked Harrison to also build her a greenhouse. A technical writer for a semiconductor firm, Harrison has an affinity for electronics, robotics, and construction. The youngest of five siblings who grew up in Corpus Christi, on the Gulf of Mexico, Harrison recalls building Radio Shack kits with their oldest brother, Randy, when he was a kid. "I have always liked to put stuff together," Harrison admits.

He first sketched a rectangular-style greenhouse with a pointed roof. A few site restraints, including setback require-

ments for the 60-by-140-foot lot and Loretta's desire to save an old bur oak, then prompted Harrison to reconsider the simple design. "The next day he brought me this elaborate drawing of a fancy, modern greenhouse," Loretta recalls. "I don't even know what he was thinking. We both love modern architecture, but I was really surprised with his sketch."

Best described as an asymmetrical, V-shaped structure with roof sections tilted at shallow angles, Harrison's greenhouse used combinations of 7-foot squares and right-angle triangles. He used a slant on the structure's south side to wrap around the oak tree and jut toward Loretta and Terrill's house.

Harrison jokes that he "reverse-engineered" the design while he built the structure. He and Loretta selected materials that fit within standard home-building parameters, including rolled-steel wall studs (the type used for office wall partitions) and 48-inch-wide panels of double-wall polycarbonate green-house sheeting. Three sliding glass doors and more than a dozen 16-inch-wide aluminum windows (typically found in mobile homes) fit seamlessly into the greenhouse framework,

ABOVE LEFT: Recirculating streams of dripping water form a delicate curtain beneath the "floor" of Loretta and Terrill's garden house. The movement creates a buffer for neighborhood noise and a visually kinetic water element. The reflection of one of Loretta's bright orange beach balls adds bold contrast to the aqua blue concrete pool. RIGHT: Come summer, Loretta moves her tropical plants outdoors, replacing them with sleek furniture and poppy orange accesso-ries. That's when she and Terrill transform the greenhouse into a warm-weather party room and pool house.

ABOVE: A band of mirrored glass mounted on a length of fencing creates for this small urban backyard an illusion of largesse. It also serves as an ever-changing mural of color, line, and form, reflecting the greenhouse, artwork, and an outdoor gravel garden.

OWNERS
Loretta and Terrill Fischer

DESIGN
ARCHITECTURE: Harrison Bates

CONSTRUCTION: Harrison Bates

LANDSCAPE: Loretta Bates Fischer, Hot Garden

INTERIOR: Loretta Bates Fischer, Hot Garden

giving Loretta a way to regulate airflow during the coldest and hottest seasons. The building's finished size—430 square feet—essentially replaces the space Loretta lost when her husband took over the garage.

The level floor rests on eleven concrete footings placed to accommodate the gradual backyard slope. But once the foundation was finished, "it was apparent that you could see right under it from inside the house," says Harrison.

The solution to this problem—a low pool of water beneath the corner entrance to the structure—is the source of an ongoing argument among Loretta, Harrison, and his best friend Sam, each of whom takes credit for its inception. "It was one of those collective eureka moments," Harrison insists. "We were all just standing there and someone said, 'You know what would be cool? How about adding a shallow pool of water?'"

The idea took hold, especially for Loretta, who yearned for a water feature. The poured concrete forms an 18-inch-deep, five-sided pool tucked partially beneath the greenhouse. Painted turquoise blue, the moatlike feature brings a much-desired liquid element into Loretta and Terrill's yard. They call it the "mini swimming pool." To continue her blue and orange motif, Loretta floats giant Day-Glo beach balls in the pool. She says, "Whether I'm sitting in it or just dangling my feet, having a pool here makes all the difference in the world. Even just visually, it cools me down."

This soothing image is reinforced by an auditory one. Dripping streams fall into the pool from PVC pipes drilled with holes and hidden beneath the elevated greenhouse. The curtain of water recirculates, its steady movement causing the plastic orange balls to rotate from one side of the pool to the other like floating sculptures. "I like the sound mask, so we can be out here talking, but the neighbors can't hear what we're saying," she jokes.

Loretta thinks about the adage "People who live in glass houses . . ." and says she is thankful that plants add an element of privacy to the translucent structure. "As soon as I filled it with my tropical plants, it was like being inside a lush jungle," she explains. "I immediately wanted to add a sitting area for my friends."

Its nighttime radiance has made this the ideal place for entertaining—from Christmas Eve soirees to summertime cocktails. "I'm always trying to think of excuses to invite our friends over so we can hang out here," Loretta says. "When they want to eat at a restaurant, I say, 'Let's get takeout.'"

MATERIALS

ROOF/WALLS: polycarbonate structured sheeting

WINDOWS: aluminum-framed

DOOR: single-insulated mill-framed sliding glass doors

FLOOR: Armstrong composite vinyl tile in Caribbean Blue and Pumpkin Orange

ABOVE: The radiant orange blooms of red yucca (*Hesperaloe parviflora*), a Texas native perennial, spice up Loretta's entry garden.

LEFT: Rolling wire racks provide flexible storage for pottery, books, supplies, and flats of young plants.

NORDIC ROOTS

CONSTRUCTED WITH OLD-WORLD JOINERY METHODS
AND EMBELLISHED WITH HAND-TOOLED MEDALLIONS
AND SPIRALS, THE OPEN-AIR SHELTER IS A FAVORITE
BACKYARD GATHERING PLACE

Leslie Lian and Ed Tuttle built a Norwegian-style home at the edge
of the Santa Cruz Mountains. They continued the architectural theme outdoors,
with an intricately carved 9-by-12-foot dining pavilion.

ABOVE: A traditional Norwegian symbol, carved by Northern California woodworkers, lends character to Leslie Lian and Ed Tuttle's dining pavilion.

OPPOSITE: After they traveled to Leslie's ancestral home near a mountainside fjord in Norway, the couple became fascinated with the *stabbur*, an agricultural building used to store grain. They adapted its timber framework and dimensions for a distinctly American purpose.

ABOVE: Positioned beneath an old oak tree on Leslie and Ed's property, the 9-by-12-foot redwood dining pavilion has a magical quality that lures them outside for fresh-air meals and parties with friends. There is a roomlike feeling to the space, with windows formed by arches and columns, a floor created by a weatherproof rug, and a roof of unkempt grass.

"When my Norwegian cousins came to visit, they admired our *stabbur* but said, 'Why would you eat in a storehouse?' Later, they sent us a Norwegian flag to fly from the top."

—LESLIE LIAN

The earthy, old-world charm of a Norwegian *stabbur* appeals to Leslie Lian and her husband, Ed Tuttle. They first saw the structure—a traditional grain-storage building—while visiting Leslie's relatives in Norway. Constructed with heavy timbers intended to last centuries, the rectangular grain-storage building rested on a raised foundation (to protect it from moisture and rodents). Its sod roof invoked the humble materials of the Scandinavian nation's agricultural heritage.

MISSION
To fashion a covered garden structure in which to dine, entertain, and relax outside

MUST-HAVES
A "green" grass roof, ceiling lanterns, radiant heaters, a trestle table with benches, an outdoor carpet, and a design that captures distant views

INSPIRATION
Modeled after a Norwegian *stabbur*, an agricultural building used to store grain or serve as an outdoor pantry

DESIGN CHALLENGES
To emulate a centuries-old Norwegian tradition but design it for a purely American function

CREATIVE SOLUTIONS
Leslie and Ed collaborated with gifted artisans to create and build a pavilion that stays true to many features of the original *stabbur* at Leslie's ancestral home in Norway: heavy timber, ornamental carvings, wide eaves, a sod roof, and a stone foundation to elevate the structure off the ground

ABOVE LEFT: A verdant ravine at the edge of Leslie and Ed's property is viewed through the *stabbur*'s two open sides. The custom-made redwood dining table and benches accommodate gatherings of friends and visiting relatives from Norway. The addition of two radiant heaters in the ceiling ensures the structure is used throughout the year. RIGHT: Master woodworker William Richter researched historical timber farm structures and authentic woodcarving patterns to build and embellish the *stabbur*. He used a spiral design to punctuate the rounded end of a supporting beam.

The couple moved to the San Francisco peninsula in 1993 and five years later embarked on a major home renovation incorporating many Nordic architectural features. And they created a *stabbur* of their own. With two open sides and a verdant sod roof, the structure has been reinterpreted as an inviting dining pavilion. Built from reclaimed redwood by a master woodworker and carved with traditional Nordic patterns, it is both a family destination and a work of art. "This is our homage to the Norwegian architecture we love," says Leslie, the daughter of Norwegian Americans. "It was our opportunity to create something authentic."

While her parents remained close to their relatives in Norway, Leslie never visited their ancestral villages until 1997. She was motivated to connect with aunts, uncles, and first cousins when her own mother, Lois Lian, was diagnosed with colon cancer.

While bittersweet due to her mother's untimely death, the experience prompted Leslie to bond with her heritage. She became enchanted with the people, places, and culture of Boggestranda, a little hamlet on the west coast of Norway, at the edge of a fjord, home to many of her mother's relatives.

On her first visit, Leslie met Gudrun, her grandmother's eighty-eight-year-old cousin, "an energetic, capable woman who could herd up ten runaway cows and who everyone went to when they needed their sod roofs repaired," she recalls. Gudrun lived at Hølvollen, a picturesque farmhouse that has been in Leslie's mother's family since the seventeenth century. "There was a tradition for the houses to be painted white, the barns to be painted red, and the storehouses, or *stabburs*, to be built in natural wood," she recalls.

The pragmatic Norwegian farm buildings bore ornamental carvings and charming details. Their character and integrity appealed to Ed, a management consultant who had studied architecture in Italy during a college year abroad. So, when he and Leslie began renovations to their 1930s cottage in Woodside, California, they wanted their home to emulate Nordic architectural elements.

Working with architect David Leavengood, Ed's stepfather, the couple transformed their original house using timber-frame construction and recycled old-growth wood. It now has a traditional Nordic-style upper floor that extends, balconylike, over the main floor. A Viking ship weather vane stands tall over the slate-tile roof. The project introduced their young sons, nine-year-old Hal and five-year-old Carl, to stories about their heritage.

When it came time to add a planned California-style covered patio off the kitchen, Leslie and Ed reconsidered. "It didn't feel like it would fit the house," Ed recalls. They brainstormed other options with their landscape designers, Roger Raiche

BELOW: Mounted above the dining table, a pair of solid brass outdoor lanterns provides illumination and atmosphere.

ABOVE: Similar to the humble farm buildings owned by Leslie's Norwegian relatives, this backyard structure has a sod roof to insulate it in cold weather and to keep things cool during the summer.

OWNER
Leslie Lian and Ed Tuttle

DESIGN
ARCHITECTURE: Paul Discoe, Joinery Structures

CONSTRUCTION/ WOODWORKING: William Richter, Joinery Structures

LANDSCAPE: Roger Raiche and David McCrory, Planet Horticulture

and David McCrory of Calistoga-based Planet Horticulture. "The two of them had the idea that the backyard would flow better if we situated a pavilion away from the house," Ed recalls. He and Leslie liked the notion of a separate structure and their landscape designers recommended that they meet with Paul Discoe of Joinery Structures, an Oakland-based contractor known for Asian timber-frame building methods.

"It turned out that even though Paul's tradition is seventeenth-century Japanese construction, he seemed to 'get' the Norwegian vernacular and understood the woodworking traditions we desired," Ed says. "Although probably some of the technical aspects of how he might have done Japanese joints were different, Paul's fundamental craft style and ethos were very consistent with what we wanted."

Ed and Leslie shared with Discoe several ideas from *Stav og Laft*, a Norwegian book that featured historic black-and-white photos and detailed drawings of timber farm structures. He enlisted woodworker William Richter, "who was just crazy enough to take on the project," Ed recalls.

Everyone involved agreed that the pavilion should be placed under the canopy of a mature oak tree on Ed and Leslie's property. Discoe located century-old redwood salvaged from a Mendocino County bridge. The beautiful old-growth wood lends a distinct character to the structure. Measuring about 11 feet tall and 9 feet wide by 12 feet long, the finished pavilion emulates some features of the original Norwegian *stabburs*. Two sides are enclosed with arched window openings, while two others remain open, giving the finished building the impression of a *stabbur* but "hybridized as a dining structure," Ed acknowledges.

Richter spent nearly two years constructing and carving the *stabbur* at Joinery Structures' Oakland shop. The woodworker embraced the project with a purity of purpose, researching authentic Norwegian wood carving and devising a special tool to cut and engineer the joinery system. The entire building is constructed with pegs and mortise-and-tenon joinery; no screws or nails were used.

"We would make these trips to Joinery Structures' workshop and find William with planes and chisels, surrounded in mountains of shavings, where our redwood structure was taking shape," Ed marvels. The columns, posts, beams, side panels, and fascia boards bear witness to his skillful woodworking. Upon close inspection, each chisel mark, groove, curve, and bevel is revealed in the vintage redwood surfaces.

Richter worked with Alef de Ghize, formerly of Joinery Structures, to complete the project, engineering the stone foundation (hidden through-bolts anchor the posts, one concession to the fact that the site is in earthquake country) and hollowing posts to accommodate wiring for ceiling heaters and lanterns and the green roof irrigation system. "They took a great deal of effort to conceal these details and make them as unobtrusive as possible," Ed adds.

Clearly fond of the pavilion's museum-quality construction, Ed and Leslie unveiled it for a gathering of friends on a rainy December evening in 2005. "Being here makes a meal very special," Ed admits. "The heaters were a good addition," Leslie concludes. Otherwise, like the Norwegians, "we'd be sitting out here cuddling up in our reindeer pelts."

MATERIALS
SOD ROOF: No-Grow grass planted on a layer of birch bark

STRUCTURE: salvaged old-growth redwood

BELOW: Resembling a legendary Viking ship and reminding the Lian-Tuttle family of Leslie's heritage, a hand-crafted weathervane is mounted on the roof of the family's Norwegian-inspired residence.

BOTTOM: Sons Hal (nine) and Carl (five) spend some silly time in their backyard *stabbur*.

LIGHT FANTASTIC

A DYNAMIC STEEL-AND-GLASS CONSERVATORY OCCUPIES THE SPOT WHERE AN AGING TOOLSHED ONCE STOOD

The modern garden structure, juxtaposed against a stately
1827 brick town house, is a brilliant backyard
destination in the heart of Manhattan.

ABOVE: A few stems are silhouetted in front of a painting by Peter Nadin. OPPOSITE: Surrounded by apartment buildings, a quiet oasis exists for the pleasure of its owners, neighbors, and friends. Designed by architect Michael Haverland, a steel-framed "shed" with a wall, doors, and a ceiling of glass feels spacious, despite the lot's narrow dimensions. Landscape designer Deborah Nevins used a serene white, green, and purple planting scheme on either side of a patterned bluestone walkway. FOLLOWING PAGE: The louvered wall system reveals (or hides) the television screen; a Shaker wood stove infuses warmth.

In 1996, Anne Kennedy and Peter Nadin did the unthinkable: they partnered with neighbors to buy two joined houses in Manhattan's Greenwich Village. "It was most unusual to buy a house with friends," Anne acknowledges. The families, whose daughters were playmates, separated the historic houses, which had been connected by interior doorways in the 1920s, and then restored them.

Four stories tall, with each floor measuring only 20 by 40 feet, the 1827 brick house was the right size for Anne, Peter, and their young daughter, Anna Page. The 20-by-60-foot backyard, which was also connected to their neighbors' yard, was generous by comparison.

MISSION
To convert a rickety wooden shed into a conservatory-like space that serves as an outdoor living room

MUST-HAVES
Glass, glass, and more glass; construction materials that relate to interior and exterior uses; built-in cabinetry to hide television, DVD player, and stereo; a woodstove and an HVAC system

INSPIRATION
Two buildings influenced the design: the Maison de Verre, a notable glass-block and steel structure completed in Paris in 1932, and a contemporary glass-and-steel-framed residence designed by architect Michael Haverland for clients in East Hampton

DESIGN CHALLENGES
To create a conservatory within tight constraints on the footprint of the origi-

nal toolshed; planning construction to allow for each piece to be delivered through the front door of the main house to the backyard site

CREATIVE SOLUTIONS
Haverland specified industrial glass block for the ceiling, giving the structure a see-through quality; the design incorporates hundreds of individual pieces of steel fastened and assembled on-site

ABOVE LEFT: Dozens of 7-inch-square industrial-glass blocks fit within a steel framework to form the roof-ceiling. RIGHT: When sunlight pours through, it casts an abstract pattern on a side table still life.

OPPOSITE, LEFT: Designer Philip Galanes selected a pair of vintage Hans Wegner rope-and-teak chairs, which are often pulled outside. The exterior of an adjacent brick building forms the "wall" for the garden. RIGHT: Clusters of white tulips and an occasional purple burst of *Camassia sp.* flourish in the garden beds.

For years, though, the adults enjoyed "outdoors" from a back porch, while Anna Page and her friends played in and around a rickety wood shed at the back of the untamed garden. "It was a great yard for ten-year-olds," Anne recalls. "The girls painted the little shed, used it as a fort, built campfires out there, and even turned it into a 'Civil War' hospital for school projects."

Once they became teenagers, Anna Page and her friends no longer used the aging shed as a playhouse. Anne and Peter knew the structure needed a face-lift. They considered repairing it and adding windows. "We were struggling about what to do with it, and I just didn't want something traditional," Anne explains. "I started to realize that I wanted a modern building, something that spoke to our house in a different way that would be more interesting than trying to do something historically accurate."

Anne, a cofounder of Art + Commerce, a New York–based agency that represents photographers, stylists, creative

directors, and artists, and Peter, a painter, author, and poet, who also lectures on art-related subjects, recalled seeing the famous 1930s-era Maison de Verre (House of Glass). "We were really inspired to see that house in the context of historic Paris," Anne says.

Through their friend and fellow bridge player Philip Galanes, the couple met architect Michael Haverland. Galanes and Haverland, who are partners, collaborate on architecture and interior design commissions. One of their projects, a modern glass-and-steel-framed residence in East Hampton, evoked the same lucent qualities that Anne admired about the Maison de Verre. "It seemed ideal to rebuild our shed entirely in glass," she recalls.

For Haverland, the notion of a greenhouse or conservatory that evokes 1940s, '50s, or '60s architecture was exciting. "It could look modern, but not trendy; anachronistic, but in context to the original town house," he says. The transformation

"It's so beautiful to be in the little house. We use it in the evenings, on Sunday afternoon when the sun pours in, in the fall when we have a fire going and the doors are open. It's heaven."

—ANNE KENNEDY

OWNERS
Peter Nadin and Anne
Kennedy

DESIGN
ARCHITECTURE: Michael
Haverland

LANDSCAPE: Deborah
Nevins, Deborah Nevins
and Associates, Inc.

INTERIOR: Philip Galanes

ABOVE: The oversize canvas by owner Peter Nadin is part of a series entitled *The First Mark*. He painted the piece using black walnut, honey, wax, indigo, cochineal, cashmere goat fleece, elderberry, and chicken eggs, most of which was grown or produced at the family's farm in the Catskills.

of an underutilized garden shed into a habitable space was possible because Haverland worked within the 11-by-20-foot parameters of its original footprint. "Because they live in a landmark district, we had to get approval from the city to take down the shed," he explains. This worked, in part, because the new glass structure is not visible from the street.

Haverland designed a steel framework engineered with commercial fittings and fasteners. Finished in a black gloss, the highly detailed structure is both industrial and elegant. The hardware, posts, and beams are intentionally exposed, "adding a level of truth about how it is made," Haverland notes.

The side and rear walls are finished in rough gray stucco, creating "a nice texture that is meant to be natural, bringing the inside-outside feeling to this space," the architect explains. In each corner, freestanding steel posts support the glass-block roof and appear to "float" inside the structure. Massive 9-foot glass doors span the entrance, hung from a ceiling track to fold open and shut, accordion style, and have 1890s antique brass handles.

Haverland selected 7-inch industrial glass blocks to create the roof. "This type of glass is clear and has a texture that refracts light, while any other structural glass looks green," he notes. During daytime, light flows through the roof, illuminating the interiors with interesting square patterns that dance across the walls, furniture, and carpet. When lit at dusk, the "glass box" takes on an alluring, translucent quality.

The 220-square-foot room accommodates a comfortable sofa, a chaise and an ottoman, and several side tables. On the west wall, custom louvered doors store board games and DVDs, and disguise television, electronics, and the HVAC system. Even though the space is winterized, Anne installed a

Shaker woodstove. "There's nothing like a little fire burning inside," she says. A timeworn tribal rug covers the floor, which is paved in bluestone and continues out to the garden.

Anne and Peter once viewed their ordinary yard from the vantage point of a covered back porch, rarely venturing farther. By adding the glass conservatory and a serene garden that links it to the main house, they feel drawn outdoors in every season, says Anne, who doesn't seem to mind as much when her schedule keeps her from leaving the city for the family's farm in the Catskills. "It's so beautiful to be in the little house. We use it in the evenings, on Sunday afternoon when the sun pours in, in the fall when we have a fire going and the doors are open," she says. "It's heaven."

Placed at a distance from the house, the conservatory is more appealing than a contiguous addition would have been, Haverland maintains. "By pulling away a 'pavilion' so that it can be viewed from the house, there is a reciprocal, visual relationship between the two places. And the garden creates an outdoor room between two pieces of architecture."

MATERIALS
ROOF/CEILING: 7-by-7-inch glass block mounted in steel framework

WALL: rough-finished stucco

WINDOWS/DOOR: track-hung custom steel-and-glass folding doors

FLOORS: bluestone pavers

BELOW: The interior view is framed by 9-foot accordion-style glass doors that slide open when the weather is nice. Gray stucco walls lend an organic counterpoint to the steel frame's industrial black gloss finish.

HEART'S CONTENT

TIM AND CAROL HICKS BOLTON RESCUED A DRAB BARN FORGOTTEN BY TIME AND FILLED IT WITH ANTIQUE FURNITURE, HUMBLE COLLECTIONS, AND A VINTAGE TRAIN SET

Where turn-of-the-twentieth-century German settlers once made

mustang grape wine, a twenty-first-century family

creates traditions of their own.

OPPOSITE: Taller than it is wide, the rugged board-and-batten exterior of a barn outside Fredericksburg, Texas, reveals its enduring character and romantic appeal. Carol Hicks Bolton and her husband, Tim Bolton, restored the century-old building and converted it to a useable outdoor retreat for their family. ABOVE: Carol finds simple beauty in the "X" and "O" design on the bottom of a weathered washtub. PAGE 207: To Carol's delight, the patina of time has mellowed her selection of textiles, wood, glass, and metal furnishings for the screened-in porch.

In 1997, the editors of *Victoria*, the magazine that delivered charms of the past to passionate and loyal readers, asked Carol Hicks Bolton, a "Designer in Residence," to decorate a room for their pages. Cocreator with her husband, Tim Bolton, of Homestead and several successful furniture and accessories shops in Fredericksburg, Texas, Carol immediately thought of the small unused barn on their 80-acre property. "It's such a precious little space; I'd always wanted to do something there," she recalls. "And the magazine gave me the encouragement to go forward."

MISSION
To decorate an "almost outside" place where parents and children can play, pretend, and daydream

MUST-HAVES
Anything old that functions nearly as well as new—vintage screen doors, rough-hewn rock flooring, cast-off furniture reupholstered with new fabrics and trims, an elderly chandelier embellished with found objects, a child's train set from the past lovingly restored for today's young hands

INSPIRATION
Carol is intrigued by the history of German immigrants who came to Texas and built their barns before building their homes. "I'm not sure if this was the case with our little barn, but it has such good bones I was inspired to fix it up just to function as a happy place."

DESIGN CHALLENGES
Carol wanted this outside room to feel as comfortable and inviting as an inside one. She also hoped to give the barn's interior a warm atmosphere although it was dominated by a model train set.

CREATIVE SOLUTIONS
Enclosing the covered porch with salvaged screen doors, using some as fixed walls and others to open wide like French doors. The interior walls are decorated with pressed flowers and the yellowed pages from train manuals.

RIGHT: Inside a 1904 barn where a family of German immigrants once made mustang grape wine, twelve-year-old Mac Bolton operates his vintage model train set.

BELOW: Intricate patchwork upholstery trimmed in old-gold chenille covers one of Carol's armchairs for her E.J. Victor furniture line and provides a cushioned nap for a resident cat. Carol's selection of distressed and carved woods and muted textiles and trims plays on the fable that each piece is more than one hundred years old.

If an armchair upholstered in single brocade is considered pretty, then Carol figures a chair finished in ten mismatched swatches is downright beautiful. "I'm just a girl who loves fabrics," she confides. Carol's penchant for thread, yarn, and floss inspired by an earlier time is evident in her signature collection of upholstered furniture produced by E.J. Victor, a North Carolina–based firm.

When Bill Hicks, Carol's father, retired as an insurance executive in the early 1970s, he dabbled in the unpainted furniture business, selling pieces at a country flea market and later opening a store called the Sawmill. Carol was still in high school when her father recruited Tim Bolton to help him learn the retail business. "He was probably only twenty, but he was a 'boy entrepreneur,'" Carol recalls with affection, describing the "older" man

"This place is one where children and animals can go in and out with reckless abandon. It may be a guesthouse someday, but for now, it's a playhouse."

—CAROL HICKS BOLTON

she knew for years as a family friend until she graduated from college and the two fell in love.

At about the same time she began to redecorate the aged backyard barn, E.J. Victor invited Carol to design a signature furniture collection. "This was great for me because it was something I could do from home," she explains.

She used a lovingly tattered design language to convert the barn into a treasured retreat for adults and children. With Tim's help, Carol cheered up the dusty building, once devoted to homemade winemaking. After clearing out the 25-by-25-foot space, they stained the walls mossy green, created an upstairs loft to accommodate an old bed (where reading or daydreaming is encouraged), and enclosed the porch with vintage screen doors.

Carol chose a faded interior palette of coral, sage, and cornhusk yellow, influenced by an old paper-covered chest and a jar of orangey red carnelian chunks that the family bought

TOP LEFT: Nine-year-old Augusta Rose snatches daydreaming time when she climbs a ladder to the sleeping loft beneath the rafters. The cozy space is decorated in her mother's signature style of tea-stained and sun-faded furnishings lovingly restored. RIGHT: An embellished pillow, part of a line that Carol and Tim sell at Homestead & Friends, their Fredericksburg shop, dresses up a frayed armchair.

ABOVE: The sunflower medallion, once part of a ceiling fixture, hangs with a bit of old needlepoint.

OWNERS
Carol Hicks Bolton and Tim Bolton

DESIGN
ARCHITECTURE: Carol Hicks Bolton and Tim Bolton

CONTRACTOR: Richard Laughlin Homes & Restoration Inc.

INTERIOR: Carol Hicks Bolton

DECORATIVE PAINTING: Thomas J. Proch & Sons

LANDSCAPE: John Webber, The Gärten

MATERIALS
ROOF: corrugated tin

EXTERIOR: board and batten

WALLS: exposed framing and wall studs stained moss green

LIGHTING: Homestead & Friends

WINDOWS: architectural salvaged French doors, cottage windows, and a diamond-paned window painted faded gold

DOOR: salvaged screen porch doors

FLOOR: native Texas stone (porch); original Texas long-leaf pine planks (barn and loft)

from a rock hound while vacationing on the Gulf Coast. "I love how the simple construction of the barn walls created perfect shelves to store and display our favorite things—model trains, photographs, and botanicals—a little of this, a little of that."

Similarly, like a magpie collecting pretty scraps and threads, she creates furniture prototypes for her Carol Hicks Bolton furniture line. Perhaps a piece begins with a Paris flea market ottoman, or an old armchair from a Texas porch. Carol adds a patchwork of jacquard, chenille, and bullion fringe to suggest it was found in her grandmother's attic.

Today, in a new studio wing of the Bolton home, a group of fellow designers works with Carol amid stacks of fabric swatches and furniture samples. While juggling phone calls to East Coast sales operations or the factory in the South, she gently urges Mac to tackle a math project or gives Augusta a reading assignment. Homeschooling goes hand in hand with putting family before business, Carol says. Like her own mother, she wants to be a hands-on parent.

After a home-cooked lunch, Carol wanders outdoors, mug of tea in hand, and bothers a sleeping cat who has commandeered a sunny spot inside the screened porch. Here, she sketches furniture ideas, plays with fabric combinations, and enjoys a moment with her children. "I still don't consider myself a working mother," Carol maintains. "I consider myself a stay-at-home mom who dabbles on the side."

TOP: Carol, Mac, and Augusta Rose enjoy a silly moment. RIGHT: Renovations to the aging barn included a salvaged diamond-pane window, a pair of hinged glass panels that open like French doors in the loft, and a patio of rough-laid native Texas stone.

OPPOSITE, LEFT: A windmill and cistern evoke the property's turn-of-the-twentieth century origins. RIGHT: Afternoon sun illuminates Carol's rosy-mauve scheme.

LIGHT BOX

IN A FOGGY CORNER OF SAN FRANCISCO, A GLOWING BLUE PAVILION IS THE PLAYFUL ANTIDOTE TO GRAY SKIES

An active family of four asked their designer to eradicate a

crumbling basketball court and replace it with

a kid- and dog-friendly urban oasis.

ABOVE: The diffusion of light through the pavilion's cobalt blue panels reveals a dreamy silhouette of roses. OPPOSITE: After slicing up the patio and basketball court that once dominated her clients' backyard, designer Shirley Alexandra Watts repurposed horizontal concrete bands to create steps and terraces. Finished with a layer of tumbled pottery, a new path leads from the residence to a contemporary Plexiglas-and-aluminum "room," an open-to-the-sky, cubelike structure with sliding doors for entry or enclosure. FOLLOWING PAGE: The pavilion is used year-round, thanks to the propane heater suspended overhead.

In 2001, Sam and Irene Pleasure and their two school-age daughters moved into a 1920s San Francisco row house with a 30-by-65-foot yard. As much as they adored the pedestrian-friendly neighborhood with its cafés, markets, and nearby parks, the family rarely spent time in their own backyard; in fact, their two dogs, Belgian Tervurens, were its principal users. Until the concrete basketball court that occupied a good portion of the space was removed, they couldn't imagine enjoying outdoor activities.

The Pleasures commissioned Bay Area garden designer and artist Shirley Alexandra Watts to turn the eyesore into an inviting retreat. She conjured a foliage-based landscape that surrounds a light-filled blue pavilion.

MISSION
To transform an unused city backyard into a series of functional—and beautiful—spaces for growing herbs, entertaining friends, and relaxing outdoors

MUST-HAVES
Bright color, privacy, and permeable surfaces that dogs won't dig up

INSPIRATION
A modern interpretation of an English folly

DESIGN CHALLENGES
There was little privacy and too much exposure to wind; a massive concrete patio/basketball court occupied 80 percent of the yard; and poor grading allowed rainfall to drain toward the home's foundation

CREATIVE SOLUTIONS
Designer Shirley Alexandra Watts sliced the concrete patio and basketball court into 12-by-48-inch bands and stacked them to form retaining walls and steps between levels of the garden. This way, no concrete had to be hauled to a landfill. The traffic areas of the garden, where dogs and people walk, is cushioned with unusual "gravel" made from tumbled porcelain chips. The attractive surface is easy to maintain and eco-friendly.

ABOVE LEFT: Irene Pleasure's collection of blue-and-white willow-patterned china lends a traditional touch to the modern environment. Here, ceramic "floats" bob in the concrete pool. RIGHT: A section of cobalt-blue Plexiglas backs the small rectangular water feature, echoing the architecture of the garden's central pavilion.

OPPOSITE, TOP: A private area for meals or an impromptu meeting is hidden on a terrace behind the pavilion. BOTTOM: The garden paths and the pavilion floor are covered with recycled bits of tumbled stoneware, an eco-friendly permeable surface. The colors and patterns are reminiscent of beach pottery.

The Richmond District, located near Golden Gate Park, is known for nearly year-round fog cover, says Sam, a physician and scientist who oversees a research lab at the University of California at San Francisco. Because they live just blocks from where the Pacific Ocean meets the mouth of San Francisco Bay, temperatures are decidedly cooler than elsewhere in the city. "There are some days in the summer where the fog never lifts until the middle of the day and it is pretty common for us to have extremely cold nights," he says.

But here's where the Pleasures, who have lived in San Francisco since the mid-1990s, found a three-story home that fit their budget and their space needs. "It's what people call an Edwardian row house," Sam says, noting the lack of a front yard and houses lined up, shoulder to shoulder, along the street.

Their 30-by-65-foot backyard, almost completely paved in concrete, was most often used by Elvis and Nico, the family pets. Grilling was out; when friends came over, the family ententertained indoors, avoiding the uninviting yard. Sam installed a basketball net in an attempt to make the patio more useful, but the family often ventured elsewhere—to Golden Gate Park or the Presidio—for their outdoor activities such as bicycling, playing soccer, and dog walking.

Sam and his wife, Irene, a scientist and lawyer who works in the biotech field, had two major complaints about their unused yard. "The patio was graded toward the house, so we had a terrible drainage problem when it rained. Plus, we were tired of how awful it looked," Sam explains. They noticed a magazine article about Bay Area garden designer Shirley Alexandra Watts, taking particular interest in the fact that she had designed a dog-friendly project.

"Shirley spent time talking with us about what we might want and thinking about what made sense here," Sam recalls. She also sketched design ideas and paged through books on modern landscapes. For her part, the designer heard more than a need to solve a landscape problem or install pretty plants. She sensed that this active family needed a reason to be lured outdoors to engage with their urban surroundings.

"I thought it was exciting to work with scientists. They have to be open to ideas and see things in ways that nobody ever perceived before," Watts says, appreciative of the way Irene and Sam embraced the possibility of nontraditional landscape—and garden structure—even though their home was anything but modern. Watts divided the Pleasures' long, narrow property into a series of interconnected rooms, much like the distinct interior spaces of their home. She solved the drainage issue by slicing the existing concrete patio into "bands," stacking pieces to form retaining walls and steps. Each of four sections of the garden is now level, stepping up to the next as the garden progresses away from the house.

"The flow between each space is not dissimilar to our house, even though the garden's style is very different," Sam points out. To further accentuate the room metaphor, Watts proposed a freestanding chamber at the heart of the garden. She hoped to give the Pleasures a separate, interior place, like the vibrant center patch of a quilt, or a room within a room.

LEFT: One of the family's two Belgian Tervuren dogs warms himself beneath a propane heater—the type usually found in hatcheries to keep chicks warm.

BELOW: The freestanding cube measures 10 by 14 feet and dominates the center of the Pleasure garden. Its sculptural presence is both beautiful and functional.

OWNERS
Sam and Irene Pleasure

DESIGN
ARCHITECTURE: Shirley Alexandra Watts, Garden Design and Installation

CONSTRUCTION: Shirley Alexandra Watts and Brendan Meyer

LANDSCAPE: Shirley Alexandra Watts

"She showed us pictures of gardens in the UK with structures that served a predominantly decorative purpose. They are called 'follies'—and they generally are thought of as useless structures," Sam says of ornamental backyard architecture—ranging from turreted huts to small-scale palaces—meant to surprise and entertain the observer. "We thought it was an interesting concept and we said, 'Go ahead and give us some ideas of what it would look like.'"

The enclosure might have been built from wood, like the fencing, except for the Pleasures' obvious interest in something modern. "I had planned to make the structure fit in with the neighborhood and use some sort of horizontal clapboard with spaces between each board, but Irene said she really wanted color," Watts explains. "So I decided to riff off the blue and white willow pattern of her ceramics collection."

She designed a sleek architectural "box" with anodized aluminum and finished it with a jolt of color—blue Plexiglas sheeting and double-wall polycarbonate (the type used in greenhouse construction) sandwiched together to form each panel. Watts filled the one-inch spaces between the panels with synthetic long-stemmed roses. As diffused light shines through the walls of the cobalt-colored enclosure, the roses—stems, leaves, and petals—are silhouetted. Like a modern twist on old-fashioned pressed flowers, the installation is unexpected and adds a playful interpretation to the conventional idea of plants in the garden. "It also hints at the floral pattern of Irene's ceramics," Watts says.

Measuring 10 by 14 feet, the aluminum-framed structure is open to the sky, allowing the Pleasures to enjoy sunny hours while still protected from ocean breezes. They can close the sliding panels for privacy and shelter, or open them for glimpses of the surrounding garden.

Putting a roof on top of the structure would have felt claustrophobic, Watts says. "It's foggy and cool here, but they are protected." Suspended from an overhead bar is a round propane heater. It is traditionally used in hatcheries to keep chicks warm, but here it is a glowing orange beacon that contrasts perfectly with the vibrant blue. The Pleasures fire up their heater on cool evenings, slide the panels tight, and enjoy temperatures 10 to 15 degrees warmer than outside the structure.

Now, guests join them for backyard barbecues (there is a hidden niche for an outdoor grill and smoker behind the structure). Their daughters bring friends outside, where they lounge on a chaise or sit near a small fountain also designed with the motif of roses between blue panels. With their outdoor perimeter enclosed by three-story houses and apartment buildings, the Pleasures once felt exposed to adjacent yards and balconies. "We used to feel surrounded, but now we enjoy privacy in our backyard," says Sam, who often brings his laptop outside to write reports. "The blue structure becomes a room of its own when you close the panels, but when they are open, you can obviously walk through it to the rest of the garden," he observes. "I like all these different configurations."

BELOW: Watts continued the blue and white pottery theme on garden paths and the floor of the structure with recycled bits of tumbled stoneware laid like gravel. The colors and patterns of broken china are reminiscent of beach pottery. She observes, "We are so close to the beach here, and the broken pottery feels appropriate."

ACKNOWLEDGMENTS

The roots of *Stylish Sheds and Elegant Hideaways* date to 2000, when Melanie Munk, features editor at *The Herald* in Everett, Washington, liked my article idea about sophisticated garden sheds and published it as "Shed Chic" in the newspaper's Home & Garden section. Soon afterward, I pitched a story about attractive backyard structures to Fred Albert, then editor of *Seattle Homes & Lifestyles*. Lucky for me, he embraced the notion, and art director Marcy Stamper assigned the shoot to Seattle architectural photographer William Wright. Bill and I met while documenting some of Seattle's coolest backyard potting sheds and garden escapes, including Sunni Rudd's barn-red studio featured on pages 50 to 57. Titled "Garden Getaways," the article ran in 2001, marking the beginning of a rewarding collaboration pairing my words with Bill's images. Since then, even while working on other book projects with other people, we couldn't ignore our mutual fascination with backyard sheds meant for higher purposes than tool storage and flowerpots.

Both of those original story ideas came from conversations with publicist and friend Cindy Combs, whose periwinkle storage shed (with trompe l'oeil nesting chickens on the door) appeared in the magazine article. Bill and I thank *Seattle Homes & Lifestyles* and later, editors at *Romantic Homes* magazine, for publishing our initial stories and photography of sheds with style.

As we began creating this book in earnest in 2005, Bill and I searched for an agent to lead us to the best publisher. Through different chapters in our lives, we have both known the talented photographer Starr Ockenga, who graciously introduced us to her agent, Barbara Hogenson. It was Barbara who suggested we meet the wonderful Sarah Jane Freymann. As our agent, Sarah Jane embraced our vision for a book about a modern interpretation of garden sheds. We thank Sarah Jane for shepherding this project from its infancy, lending us positive support, advice, and motivation. She is a gift.

As we prepared the book proposal, we turned to our friend and former *Seattle Homes* art director Marcy Stamper. She also believed in our ideas and thoughtfully designed the initial visual concepts that accompanied our book proposal. We are forever grateful to her.

In the hands of our intuitive and big-thinking editor, Doris Cooper, and the imminently gifted art director, Marysarah Quinn, at Clarkson Potter, this book has journeyed from a seed of an idea to a beautiful reality. We are so grateful for their belief in and enthusiasm for *Stylish Sheds*, especially during a brutal production schedule. They made this dream a reality!

One of the first questions we are asked about this book is: How did you find the sheds to include? Our answer: *Shed Angels*. Without the often spontaneous and unexpected help from the following friends and colleagues, we could not have found the inspiring locations featured on these pages, or have so smoothly produced these chapters while "on location." These *Shed Angels* supported us in many ways, including helping us find amazing sheds, feeding, housing, and transporting us, lending supplies and generally cheering us on! Our heartfelt gratitude goes to each of them: John Akers, Susan Wittig Albert, Sara Anderson, Gregory Bader, Harrison Bates, Sydney Baumgartner, Abby Jane Brody, Jennifer Calvo, Robyn and Don Cannon, Doris Cooper, Cindy Combs, Robin and Paul Cowley, Shira and Irv Cramer, Francine Day, Charles Dean, David Ellis, Jennifer Ferri, Nancy and Catherine Finnerty, David Friesen, Alejandro Gamundi, Christina Glynn, Betsy and Harald Hansen, Susan Harkavy, Michael Haverland, Gail Hongladarom,

Darlene Huntington, Alicia Indorante, Randolph Keller, Linda Knutson, Linda Lehmus-virta, Daniel Lowery, Shane Lyle, Gillian Mathews, Suzie Humphreys Mayo, Jane Milford, J.C. Nelson, Ellen Spector Platt, Susan Prince, Anita and Fred Prinzing, Emily Reaman, Paula Refi, Bernadine and Jean-Paul Richard, Mary Rodriguez, Karen Roth, Ben and Laurie Ryan, Ryan Grey Smith, David Spence, Tom Spencer, Marian Sprague, Fred Strauss, Gregory Thomas, Louis Truesdell, Richard Turner, Skip Wachsberger, Phyllis Wender, Stacey Winnick, Will and Nancy Wright, and Thomas Zachary.

A group of rare individuals infused joy into this book's creative journey. They include Paula Panich, who shared her mountain-writing retreat when I was desperate for a quiet week to work on the manuscript; Judy Bradley, who planned and escorted me on a day-long "shed scouting" tour in San Diego; Anne Marie Van Nest, who twice shared time, lodging, transportation, and her fabulous Austin hospitality; and Wendy Bassett, who found locations, fed, and "mothered" us, making everything in Atlanta come together effortlessly. We cherish each of you.

Bill and I owe the greatest of thanks to the owners of these wonderful locations. They woke up before dawn to hand us steaming mugs of coffee and tea, let us rearrange their furniture and possessions, posed for portraits, fed us homemade fare, and even gave us lodging. This book is wonderful because of the friendships we've forged with each. Thank you to Patrick Anderson and Les Olson, Rand Babcock and Tony Nahra, John Barham, John Bernatz and Joseph Marek, Amy Bloom, Carol Hicks Bolton and Tim Bolton, Joan Enticknap, Loretta and Terrill Fischer, Janie and Billy Fowler, Lani and Larry Freymiller, Kathy and Ed Fries, Edgar Lee, Liz Lyons Friedman and John Gavrilis, Jennie and Tully Hammill, Anne Kennedy and Peter Nadin, Leslie Lian and Ed Tuttle, Brenda and Gerald Lyle, Terry and Dave Maczuga, Mary Martin, Martha and Ray Mendoza, Irene and Sam Pleasure, Sunni and Joel Rudd, Lin Su, Beverly and Eldon Sutton, Betty Wasserman, Shirley Alexandra Watts, Sylvia and Steven Williams, and Michelle and Rob Wyles.

Even though not every property we visited and photographed appears in this final form, we appreciate the kindnesses of every shed owner we met.

During the course of this project, Bill and his wife, Pauline Ashman, celebrated the birth of their daughter, Ella Margaret Wright. I moved with my husband, Bruce Brooks, and sons Benjamin and Alexander Brooks, from Seattle to Southern California. These major life events are challenging and intense, but with the added insanity of our yearlong photography and travel and writing marathon, we're enormously grateful for their love and support. Without them, this book would still be nothing more than an idea.

We will continue to share our discoveries, stories, photographs, and new stylish shed resources at our website blog, www.shedstyle.com. Please visit!

Debra Prinzing,
www.debraprinzing.com
William Wright,
www.williamwrightphoto.com

RESOURCES

Many items pictured but not listed are from private collections.

STUCCO STUDIO (PAGE 15)
Architectural and landscape design: Joseph Marek, 2252 25th Street, Santa Monica, CA 90405, 310-399-7923, www.josephmarek.com.
Furnishings: vintage metal chairs upholstered in lime green Sunbrella fabric(exterior); desks custom-designed by Joseph Marek. **Artwork:** Vintage Jeré metal sculpture.

THE NEWSROOM (PAGE 22)
Contractor: Daniel Aguirre, Santa Cruz, CA.
Furnishings: desk from www .craigslist.com. **Artwork:** "Iwo Jima" photograph, signed by the late AP photojournalist Joe Rosenthal. Martha Mendoza's articles can be read at www.ap.org.

PERSONAL SPACE (PAGE 24)
Architect: Kemp Mooney, Kemp Mooney Architects, 30 Polo Drive NE, Atlanta, GA 30309, 404-815-9561, fkmooney@bellsouth.net. **Architectural consultant:** David Jenkins, Continental Hardware, 678-207-7170.
Landscape design: David Ellis, Ellis Landesign, P.O. Box 52031, Atlanta, GA 30355, 404-261-8488, ellislandesign@aol.com. **Stonework:** Mike Norris and Sandy Simmons.
Furnishings: Mary's Garden sign hand-painted by Mary Martin on 1920s milk glass; custom-framed by Myott Studio, www.myottstudio.com; silver tray, champagne bucket, flutes, and dishes from the family collection; Joggling board from the Old Charleston Joggling Board Co., 652, King Street, P.O. Box 20608, Charleston, SC 29413, 843-723-4331.
Mary's Garden Champagne Savers, P.O. Box 12320, Atlanta, GA 30355, 404-355-4431 or 877-220-2214, www.mgarden.com. Also available at select Neiman Marcus locations and at Bergdorf Goodman.

WORDPLAY (PAGE 32)
Contractor: Roger Bryson, 860-663-2131
Furnishings: pine window seat and desk custom-built by Roger Bryson.

Read more about Amy Bloom and excerpts of her work at: www .amybloom.com.

A GARDEN GALLERY (PAGE 41)
View Liz Lyons Friedman's artwork at: www.aptosartshoppe.com. Visit Liz Lyons Friedman's studio and more than 250 other artist studios at the Open Studios Art Tour, sponsored by the Cultural Council of Santa Cruz County, held during several weekends each September and October. For more details, call 800-833-3494 or visit www.santacruzevents.travel.

REC ROOM (PAGE 48)
Architect: Ryan Grey Smith, Modern-Shed, 5136 NE 54th Street, Seattle, WA 98105, (206) 524-1188, www.modern-shed.com. **Construction:** Modern-Shed. **Interior design:** Lin Su, lin@linsu.com. **Landscape design:** Peter Wishinski, Ganesa Garden Design, 323-841-5698, www.ganesagarden design.com.
Furnishings: shelves, deck chair, side table, bookcase from Ikea, 800-434-4532, www.ikea-usa.com; indoor chair from West Elm, 888-922-4119, www .westelm.com. **Artwork:** *The Circus*, painting by Lin Su, lin@linsu.com.

ART AND SOUL (PAGE 50)
Architectural design: Norm Steelhammer and Sunni Rudd. **Construction:** Norm Steelhammer, Joel Rudd. **Landscape design:** Sunni Rudd. **Artwork:** Sunni Rudd's illustrated greeting cards are available through Aunt Coco's Cottage, P.O. Box 78688, Seattle, WA 98178-0688, 206-268-0514. www.auntcocoscottage.com.

SUNCATCHER (PAGE 61)
Architectural, interior, and landscape design: Michelle Wyles, Garden Dance, 25 North Front Street, #3, Yakima, WA 98901, 509-452-0611, www.rosegarden farm.com. **Contractor/builder:** Gale Curtis, 607 South Second Street, Yakima, WA 98901.
Furnishings: Japanese rain barrel dining table base, and imported teak folding chairs from David Smith & Co., 1107 Harrison Street, Seattle, WA 98109, 206-223-1598, www.david smithco.com (66-inch round top made

from double-thick plywood with whitewash stain), 1940s kitchen/potting bench sink from Seattle Building Salvage, 425-374-2550, www.seattlebuildingsalvage.com; salvaged Gothic barn windows, Rosebud Antiques, Coeur d'Alene, Idaho. **Artwork:** antique cast-stone sheep, antique chicken carousel figure, and vintage scale from Michelle and Rob's private collection; McCoy pottery from Michelle's private collection.

SUBURBAN FOLLIES (PAGE 69)
Designer/builder: John Akers custom orders through Gillian Mathews, Ravenna Gardens, 206-749-9761, www.ravennagardens.com.
Furnishings: live chickens from Murray McMurray Hatchery, 800-456-3280, www.mcmurrayhatchery.com; vintage farm implements and chicken-themed items, Kathy Fries's personal collection.

PLANTING PARADISE (PAGE 77)
Architect: Gregory Bader, AIA, Bader Architecture, 752 Harvard Avenue East, Seattle, WA 98102, 206-344-3878, www.baderarch.com. **Contractor:** Mike Adams, Adams Construction Services, 11027 118th Place Northeast, Kirkland, WA 98033, 425-827-9447, www.adamsconsvc.com. **Landscape design:** Tom Zachary and Francine Day, Tom Zachary Landscape Architects, 5337 Ballard Avenue NW, Seattle, WA 98107, 206-789-5645.
Materials: copper roof by Ballard Sheet Metal, 4763 Ballard Avenue Northwest, Seattle, WA 98107, 206-784-0545, www.ballardsheetmetal.com; finial by Wind and Weather, 800-922-9463, www.windandweather.com; locally salvaged brick and Clinker brick from Gavin Historical Bricks, 2050 Glendale Road, Iowa City, Iowa 52245, 319-354-5251, www.historicalbricks.com; doors by Simpson Door Co., 400 Simpson Avenue, McCleary, WA 98557, 800-952-4057, www.simpsondoor.com; windows by Pella Windows, 800-374-4758, www.pella.com.
Furnishings: potting bench from Cost Plus World Market, 877-967-5362, www.worldmarket.com; vintage garden tools: Joan Enticknap's personal collection.

HAMPTON HUT (PAGE 84)
Construction: Arthur Peterson, 141 Altmar Avenue, West Islip, New York, 11795.

HILL COUNTRY HAVEN (PAGE 93)
Builder/contractor: Brad McCasland and Paul Solis.
Materials: doors/windows by Sherry Landers, Mint Creek Farms, 1418 County Road 323A, Liberty Hill, Texas 78642.

A ROOM WITH A VIEW (PAGE 100)
Architectural design: Randolph Scott Keller, ASLA Landscape Architecture, 206-782-1521, www.rskasla.com.
Construction/carpentry/landscape design: Jennie Hammill, Ballard Woodworks, 206-783-5952, jennifer@hammills.com.
Materials: exterior paint by Benjamin Moore "Kendall Charcoal" HC-166, interior paint by Miller Paint "Soft Gold" with double pigment; tumbled concrete "Autumn" pavers from Home Depot.
Furnishings: bench/daybed, bird mosaic table, and end table custom-designed and built by Jennie Hammill.
Artwork: wooden carved bird sculptures by Seattle artist Michael Zitka, available through Lucca Great Finds, 5332 Ballard Avenue NW, Seattle, WA 98107, 206-782-7337, www.luccastatuary.com.

HEART OF THE COUNTRY (PAGE 109)
Construction: Johnny Fowler, International General Contractors, 425-417-3104. Water wheel/dry creek by Nick Sands, Nature's Way Landscape and Design, 425-377-8444.
Janie and Billy Fowler have collected and salvaged building materials and architectural fragments from the following sources: The Original Round Top Antiques Fair, Round Top, Texas, 512-237-4747, www.roundtoptexasantiques.com; Craven Farm Inc., 13817 Short School Road, Snohomish, WA 98290, 360-568-2601, www.cravenfarm.com.

SWEET RETREAT (PAGE 118)
Architectural design: Rand Babcock, Legacy Creations, 206-286-1827, rand@legacycreations.com.

Landscape design: Daniel Lowery, Queen Anne Gardens, 206-285-6770, www.queenannegardens.com.
Furnishings: daybed from Corsican Furniture Co., 800-421-6247, www.corsican.com; coverlet from Cost Plus World Market, 877-967-5362, www.worldmarket.com; marble table from Fine's Gallery, 11400 South Cleveland Avenue, Fort Meyers, Florida, 33907, 239-277-0009 or 866-860-1710, www.finesgallery.com; linen draperies from Restoration Hardware, 800-910-9836, www.restorationhardware.com; exterior sconces from Stone Manor Lighting, 6219 Porterdale Road, Malibu, CA 90265, 888-534-0544, www.stonemanorlighting.com.

EXTRAVAGANT GESTURE (PAGE 127)
Materials: finial by International Terra Cotta Inc., 690 North Robertson Boulevard, Los Angeles, CA 90069, 310-657-3752 or 800-331-5329; paint by Dunn-Edwards, 4885 East 52nd Place, Los Angeles, CA 90040, 888-337-2468, www.dunnedwards.com (pavilion: "Golden Retriever"; trim: "Denali Green,"); lighting by Corbett Lighting Co., 14625 East Clark Avenue, City of Industry, CA 91745, 626-336-4511, www.corbettlighting.com; tile by Coronado Stone Products, 11191 Calabash Avenue, Fontana, CA 92337, 800-847-8663, www.coronado.com.
Furnishings: iron furniture from O. W. Lee Co., 1822 E. Francis Street, Ontario, CA 91761, 800-776-9533, www.owlee.com; teak bench from Smith & Hawken, 800-940-1170, www.smithandhawken.com.

SOUTHERN COMFORT (PAGE 135)
Construction: Strathmore Floors–Design–Cabinets, 50 East Great Southwest Parkway, Atlanta, GA 30336, 404-872-0024, www.strathmorefloors.com. **Landscape design:** Kathy Montgomery, Kathy Montgomery & Associates, 1522 Huber Street Northwest, Suite A, Atlanta, GA 30318, 404-746-3582, kmagardens@bellsouth.net.
Flooring: Strathmore Floors–Design–Cabinets.
Birdhouses: Some of the birdhouses featured are from Boxwoods Gardens and Gifts, 100 E Andrews Drive, Atlanta, Georgia 30305, 404-233-3400.

COTTAGE COURTYARD (PAGE 142)
Furnishings: wall fountain: Garden Stone Antiques, 5171 Santa Fe Street, San Diego, CA 92109, 858-272-8722; area rug from Rug Weavery, 353 Glenmont Drive, Solana Beach, CA 92075, 858-755-4451; bell, mirror, and table from the Village Consignment, 202 North Cedros, Solana Beach, CA 92075, 858-847-0345; wicker wine bottles from Del Mar Antique Show, Del Mar, CA; gray pottery from Feather Acres Nursery, 980 Avocado Place, Solana Beach, CA 92075, 858-755-3093; English pottery from Garden Stone Antiques; basket from Mon Petit Chou, 1279 Santa Fe Drive, Encinitas, CA 92024, 760-402-7606.

POETIC LICENSE (PAGE 150)
Architectural design: Shirley Alexandra Watts, Garden Design and Installation, 1000 Park Street, Alameda, CA 94501, 510-521-5223, www.sawattsdesign.com.
Materials: tile pavers by American Soil Products, 2121 San Joaquin Street, Richmond, CA, 510-292-3000, www.americansoil.com; benches and fountain custom-designed and fabricated by Shirley Alexandra Watts, Garden Design and Installation.
Pottery: Carmelo Milone terra-cotta available through American Soil Products.

CREEK HOUSE (PAGE 153)
Salvaged building materials from the Re-Store, 2309 Meridian Street, Bellingham, WA 98225, 360-647-5921, www.re-store.org.
Many of the native plants and orchard trees come from Cloud Mountain Farm and Nursery, 6906 Goodwin Rd. Everson, WA 98247, 360 966-5859, www.cloudmountainfarm.com.
Learn more about the Nooksack Salmon Enhancement Association, a community-based nonprofit organization dedicated to restoring sustainable wild salmon runs in Whatcom County at www.n-sea.org.

SECOND ACT (PAGE 161)
Architect: Glenn Leitch, Highland Associates, 228 East 45th Street, New York, NY 10010, 212-681-0200, highlandassociates.com. **Contractor:** Home Design, Westhampton, NY.
Interior design: Betty Wasserman Art and Interiors, 212-352-8476, www

.betterywasserman.com. **Landscape design:** Harmonia, East Hampton, NY. **Furnishings:** custom furniture from Betty Wasserman, 212-352-8476, www.bettyhome.com; Japanese paper light sculpture from John Wigmore Lighting Designs, 5–22 46th Avenue, 3rd floor, Long Island City, NY 11101, 718-389-9110, www.johnwigmore.com. **Artwork:** Betty Wasserman Art & Interiors; photograph series by Lisa Ross; paintings by Melinda Stickney Gibson and Louise Crandell; photographs of Milly by Betty Wasserman.

ISLAND IDYLL (PAGE 168)
Design/construction: John Akers custom orders through Gillian Mathews, Ravenna Gardens, 206-749-9761, www.ravennagardens.com. **Furnishings:** antique French marble-topped cast-iron table and icons from Edgar Lee's private collection; candles from Votivo Ltd., www.votivo.com.

BACKYARD ZEN (PAGE 170)
Architect: Gregory Thomas, AIA, CG&S Design-Build, 402 Corral Lane, Austin, TX 78745, 512-444-1890, Gregory.thomas@cgsdb.com. **Landscape design:** Fred Strauss, Thrive/Inside-Out, 512-567-8732, www.thriveaustin.com. **Contractor:** David Wilkes and Philip Perry, Trinity Builders, P.O. Box 50276, Austin, TX 78763, 512-453-4982, www.trinitybuildersaustin.com. **Stonemason:** Lupe Rios, Rio Verde Landscaping, 190 Tiffany Trail, Austin, TX 78719, 512-789-6610. **Sculpture:** *Hands on Hip*, bronze figure by sculptor Jim Corbin, Kansas City.

MOD POD (PAGE 181)
Architectural designer/builder: Harrison Bates, 2933 East 14th Street, Austin, TX 78702, 512-560-9501, harrison.bates@cirrus.com. **Interior/landscape design:** Loretta Bates Fischer, Hot Garden, 512-771-4319, loretta@nfainc.com. **Materials:** polycarbonate structured sheeting by Polygal USA, www.polygalusa.com, ordered through Austin Plastics & Supply, 2415 Kramer Lane, Austin, TX 78758, 512-836-1025; windows: Ashville Mobile Homes, 36235 US Hwy 231, Ashville, AL 35953, 800-979-2647, www.ashvillemobilehomes.com; doors by Lowe's (special order), 800-445-6937, www.lowes.com; Armstrong composite vinyl tile floor

from Home Depot, 800-553-3199, www.homedepot.com; custom stainless support brackets and removable steps by Central Machine Works, 4824 East Cesar Chavez Street, Austin, TX 78702, 512-385-3287. **Furnishing:** "Sevilla" reproduction mid-century modern chairs from Garden Ridge, 5151A U.S. Highway 290 West, Austin, TX 78735, 512-892-3059, www.gardenridge.com; drum-shape paper shade by Cultural Intrigue, 800-799-7422, www.culturalintrigue.com; terra-cotta pots painted "Evening Hush" gray, Behr Paint.

NORDIC ROOTS (PAGE 188)
Architecture/design: Paul Discoe, Joinery Structures, 2500 Kirkham Street, Oakland, CA 94607, 510-451-6345, www.joinerystructures.com. **Construction/woodworking:** William Richter, Joinery Structures. **Landscape design:** Roger Raiche and David McCrory, Planet Horticulture, 3485 Old Lawley Toll Rd, Calistoga, CA 94515, 415-827-4342, www.planethorticulture.com. **Materials:** roof grass by No-Mow Grass, 866-666-6947, www.nomowgrass.com; ceiling heaters by Infratech, 344 West 157th Street, Gardena, CA 90248, 310-354-1250 or 800-421-9455, www.infratech-usa.com. **Lanterns:** "Westwind" by Hinkley Lighting, 800-446-5539, www.hinkleylighting.com. **Furnishings:** Redwood dining table and benches custom-made by Jim Simons, Vintage Redwood Co., 122 Green Oaks Drive, Visalia, CA 93277, 559-733-5613, www.vintageredwoodcompany.com; table linens by Yves Delorme, 800-322-3911, www.yvesdelorme.com; plates from Restoration Hardware, 800-910-9836, www.restorationhardware.com; tumblers from Crate and Barrel, 800-967-6696, www.crateandbarrel.com; spiral candles from Sundance catalogue, 800-422-2770, www.sundancecatalog.com; "Rosemaling" hand-painted fruit bowl by Julie Anne Droivold, 530-265-9046, julieanne44@hotmail.com.

LIGHT FANTASTIC (PAGE 197)
Architecture: Michael Haverland Architect, PC, One Union Square West, Suite 810, New York, NY 10003, 212-780-9188, www.michaelhaverland.com. **Construction:** Damo Construction. **Interior design:** Philip Galanes, www.galaneshaverland.com. **Landscape**

design: Deborah Nevins, Deborah Nevins & Associates Inc., 270 Lafayette Street, Suite 903, New York, NY 10012, 212-925-1125. **Furnishings:** Edward Wormley sofa, purchased on eBay, slip-covered in white cotton twill; vintage Hans Wegner chaise/ottoman and vintage Hans Wegner rope and teak chairs; private collection; vintage Eames screen from reGeneration Modern Furniture, 38 Renwick Street, New York, NY 10013, 212-741-2102, www.regenerationrurniture.com. **Artwork:** *The First Mark*, a series by Peter Nadin, www.peternadin.com.

HEART'S CONTENT (PAGE 205)
Furnishings: furniture, vintage accessories, and antiques from Homestead and Friends, 230 East Main Street, Fredericksburg, TX 78624, 830-997-5551, www.homesteadstores.com; Carol Hicks Bolton custom furniture and lighting from www.carolhicksbolton.com. Carol Hicks Bolton furniture is available from E.J. Victor, 110 Wamsutta Mill Road, P.O. Box 309, Morganton, NC 28680-0309, 828-437-1991, www.ejvictor.com.

LIGHT BOX (PAGE 212)
Architectural/landscape design: Shirley Alexandra Watts, Garden Design and Installation, 1000 Park Street, Alameda, CA 94501, 510-521-5223, www.sawattsdesign.com. **Construction:** Shirley Alexandra Watts and Brendan Meyer. **Beach pottery:** Building Resources, 701 Amador Street, San Francisco, CA 94124, 415-285-7814, www.buildingresources.org. **Fountain:** custom-design by Shirley Alexandra Watts, Garden Design and Installation. **Furnishings:** table and "lounge" blue chaise from Concreteworks Gallery, 1137 57th Avenue, Oakland, CA 94621, 510-534-7141, www.concreteworks.com; "air chair" from Design Within Reach, 800-944-2233, www.dwr.com.

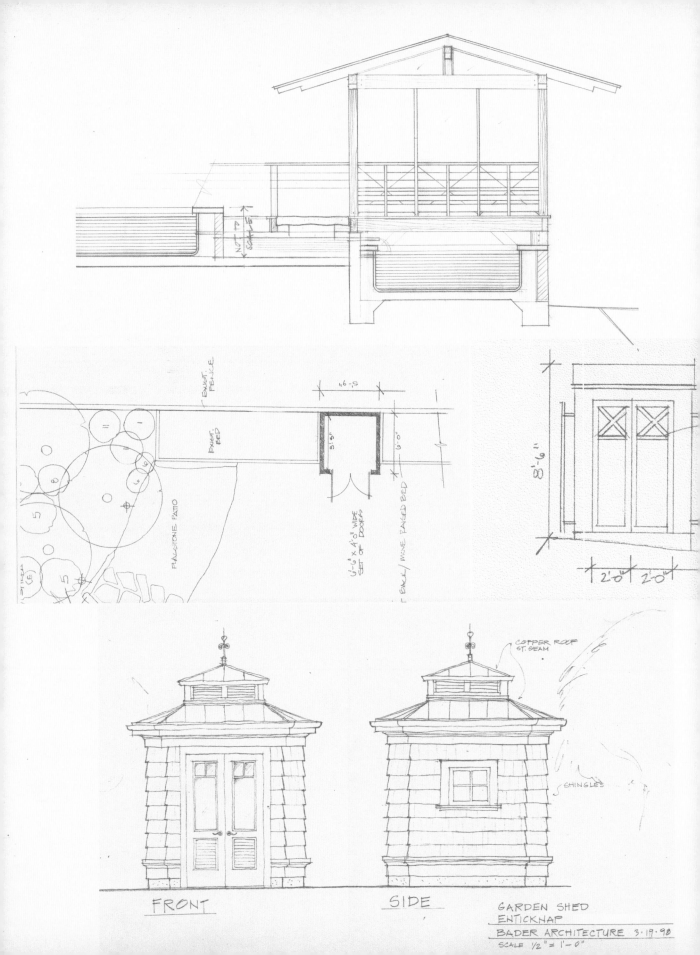

FRONT

SIDE

GARDEN SHED
ENTICKNAP
BADER ARCHITECTURE 3·19·98
SCALE 1/2" = 1'-0"